D0706749

Recent Titles in
The Entrepreneur's Guide

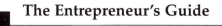

The Entrepreneur's Guide

CJ Rhoads, Series Editor

The Entrepreneur's Guide to Mastering the Inner World of Business

Nanci Raphael

Foreword by Marshall Goldsmith

PRAEGER

AN IMPRINT OF ABC-CLIO, LLC
Santa Barbara, California • Denver, Colorado • Oxford, England

Library of Congress Cataloging-in-Publication Data

Raphael, Nanci.
    The entrepreneur's guide to mastering the inner world of business / Nanci Raphael ;
foreword by Marshall Goldsmith.
        p. cm. — (The entrepreneur's guide)
    Includes bibliographical references and index.
        ISBN 978–0–313–38002–0 (hard copy : alk. paper) — ISBN 978–0–313–38003–7 (ebook)
1. Entrepreneurship. 2. Success in business. I. Title.
HB615.R367   2010
658.4′21—dc22   2010011190

ISBN: 978–0–313–38002–0
EISBN: 978–0–313–38003–7

14 13 12 11 10   1 2 3 4 5

This book is also available on the World Wide Web as an eBook.
Visit www.abc-clio.com for details.

Praeger
An Imprint of ABC-CLIO, LLC

ABC-CLIO, LLC
130 Cremona Drive, P.O. Box 1911
Santa Barbara, California 93116-1911

This book is printed on acid-free paper ∞

Manufactured in the United States of America

This book is dedicated to my children, Andrew, Jessica, and Kimberly, who continue to teach me about love and life.

Business is your highest spiritual understanding demonstrated.

Neale Donald Walsch

Contents

Foreword

We are living in a new era—one of rapid change, uncertainty, and global competition. In this new era, the message of *The Entrepreneur's Guide to Mastering the Inner World of Business* is becoming more and more important. As job security fades into yesterday and global competition creates change, challenge, and opportunities, we all need to think like entrepreneurs. We need to learn to do what successful entrepreneurs know how to do so well: compete, innovate, handle stress, and more.

As an entrepreneur it is easy to take on more than humanly possible—who else will do it? As an entrepreneur it is easy to rest on success—why change it if it's working? There are times of hyper-activity and periods of inactivity. The list of these extremes is practically infinite! It can be difficult to achieve balance with this seeming roller-coaster ride of a professional life—and with so much to do and so little time, who could smooth out the ride anyway? To survive and thrive, leaders have to face the reality that when managing the Inner World of Business, they face serious and debilitating burnout.

This book is filled with great stories of successful entrepreneurs, but it's far more than that! As you read the stories, think about your own life. How can you apply the lessons in this book to your own entrepreneurial endeavor? Ask yourself the questions at the end of the chapters. Practice the tools that you will find there, such as:

> Let go! Pushing harder for a solution isn't the answer. Lighten your grip and let the answers come to you.
> Rid yourself of the blame game: There is no room for growth or progress with blame in the way.
> Become accountable. Take ownership. Change your perspective from *you* to *I*.
> Use the 5,000-year-old business tool: Learn to meditate. It may help you improve self-awareness, solve problems, and reduce stress.

Enjoy this book, and use it to help you have a wonderful career and a great life!

Marshall Goldsmith

New York Times best-selling author of *What Got You Here Won't Get You There* and winner of the Harold Longman Award—Best Business Book of 2007. His most recent book is *Mojo: How To Get It, How To Keep It, How To Get It Back If You Lose It.*

Acknowledgments

This was the book that I had been thinking about for years. It lay dormant inside of me for a long time. There were many people who helped me to get this book out of my head and onto paper. Dr. Wayne Dyer was one of them. Through his writings, he brought me so many gifts about managing life's obstacles, being your true self, and going for what you want with a quiet internal knowing. He told me that if I could think it, then the book was already there. When I was ready, it would begin to flow. He was right.

Marshall Goldsmith kicked my butt (in a nice way) and told me to write it. I kept hearing his words on those difficult days when my creativity was strangled with deadlines.

There was another monumental person involved in the birth of this book, Ed Claflin, an agent and brilliant editor. He is a remarkable individual who I hope to collaborate with on future projects.

Anne Browning coached this book out of me. With her encouragement, I connected to my purpose in writing this book, which kept me motivated. I will always be grateful for Anne's remarkable insight and compassion.

Dr. Dan Gottlieb helped me to understand the connection between pain and compassion. He is one of the gentlest souls in this world, and also one of the wisest.

My husband and best friend, Art Bernstein, has always supported my life's work. He still tells the story of remembering my closet walls when we first met. They were adorned with posted pictures of my dreams. Every time I walked into my closet, my dreams became a reality—showing me what was possible. I think he wanted to see how this would all turn out. Art encouraged me with comments of how I was destined for this path, as I moved from employee to entrepreneur. When I forgot, he reminded me of my purpose. Through the emotional and financial ups and downs of running a business, he was always by my side. My love runs forever deep.

My parents, Jackie and Erwin Raphael, always lent an ear when I wanted to read a chapter or paragraph out loud. Their words of support were consistent and filled with love and pride. It is because of their early belief in me, their love, and their values that I had the confidence to go for my dreams.

My children, Andy, Jessica, and Kimberly; my daughter-in-law, Courtney; and my granddaughter, Hannah, each bring a unique dimension to my life, filled with many riches. Many of the lessons I have learned and teach my clients have come from being a parent.

The list is long, but I'd like to thank all the wonderful folks at Praeger and ABC-CLIO Publishers for their belief in the importance of this book and their commitment to it. My deepest appreciation goes to CJ Rhoads and Jeff Olson for accepting my manuscript and Bob Everett who introduced us. CJ's editorial guidance was like that of a great coach, motivating and direct. I also want to thank Valentina Tursini for her editing and production assistance, and Brian Romer.

And most importantly, I want to thank all of my wonderful clients, past and present. It is because of you, and your desire to be the best that you can be, that this book was written. I love you with all my heart.

Introduction: Being an Entrepreneur

I must have come out of the womb with the word *ENTREPRENEUR* stamped on my forehead. Was I programmed at birth? Perhaps. All I know is, I have always had a fervor for venture. For some reason—perhaps embedded in my DNA—I need the freedom to cultivate my own course, innately fighting against conventional rules.

So . . . ever since the earliest stage of my career, what I've done is contemplate, start up, and run companies. Then once running, I reinvent them while reinventing myself. It's a way, I suppose, to keep me interested and excited about my pursuit. That seems to be a large part of my job description. And not always an ideal job, by any measure. While I've risen, at times, to glorious heights where anything seems possible, I've also descended into gloomy caverns of disappointment.

Oh, and did I mention the landmines? No different than you, I imagine, I've stepped on many. And although I've walked away physically intact, each landmine blew up my current thinking, my current beliefs, and dropped me on my nose. I was forced to take a closer, harder look at where I was going, what I *really* wanted, and to inquire more deeply into just who I was.

But the rewards—ahh, the rewards. Those are what lure me on and, in the toughest times, encourage me to hold on—like other entrepreneurs, this is what we do. Just when we really need it, especially when the obstacles seem greatest, we remember who we are—risk takers, survivors, business drivers. We have dreams to fulfill. And rewards to gather. Eventually, the storms pass.

Let's face it; the inner world of an entrepreneur is as ever-changing as the weather. Time and again we are reminded that nothing is stable. Now, after decades of coaching and consulting with other entrepreneurs, I can tell you that nearly all of us go through similar storms and upheavals. There is one sure constant—just as we start to settle in and get comfortable; the winds begin to stir once more.

Several years ago, when I was running my nearly 10-year-old consulting company, I hit a low point that would evolve into a time of great introspection—further learning about myself and my commitment as an entrepreneur.

The problem occurred when my company had become quite successful. For years, the business had grown and grown. But then it hit a wall. It got stuck.

If you're an entrepreneur, you know what this feels like. You wrestle with all kinds of thoughts, and can't quite figure out what's wrong. In my case, I wondered, "Was it the economy? 9/11? The need for a new business model?" I tried all sorts of methods to boost my company, and nothing seemed to work. I began pumping money into the business, but it was a bottomless pit.

My gut was saying, "This is it. It's time to say good-bye. Now, let go and move on!"

Overwhelmed with the enormity of the decision, I finally stopped wrestling with it and listened to my gut. I did let go. I let go of the company to which I had given birth. It was one of the hardest things I ever had to do. It took a great deal of strength and courage for me to say good-bye to what I'd been building all those years. It was the entity that was always in the forefront of my mind. Perhaps some thought I was making a mistake, but I knew it was time. I had to follow my gut and my heart—to take the step deemed necessary.

The following few months seemed like a period of mourning. The soul of my business lived on inside of me, but I had no office to go to. I took shelter from the aftermath of my difficult decision, sitting in a chair, reading or meditating, or staring out the window wondering what was going to happen from here.

It took many months to go full circle and complete the transition of running a vibrant business to wondering what was next. That transition period was important. It helped me formulate thoughts and recreate dreams. When I looked inside, I saw that the one thing I couldn't let go of was my purpose and passion for what I wanted to continue to do—helping others grow their businesses and gain financial freedom, while finding more meaning and happiness in their lives—and that I had needed to take this uncertain course myself to reconnect to it. Therefore, the next thing I knew I would do was to start up another company. But this would be different. I had learned much from my previous business. Most importantly, I wanted to have more fun, more balance, and less stress. And that is exactly what I have—an evolving business that is now a global company where I am hired by high-achieving go-getters (business owners and business leaders) to help them break through barriers so that they can achieve higher levels of income, revenue, and profit, have more meaning and happiness, and have a greater impact in the world.

So how does this entrepreneurial spirit get in your blood? Where does it begin? My family included a long line of entrepreneurs, so for me, the first entrepreneurial classroom was the dinner table. I learned early on from my family business that happiness is as elusive as success. Victories, though exciting, are short lived. Failures are recurring, and with each failure comes frustration and disappointment.

Now that I can look back over my own experience, I see that those kitchen-table lessons were the template for my future. As with my family, I too have savored the sweetness of achievement and become familiar with the sting of regret.

Like my parents and grandparents, I have never been able to take the path of the perceived *safe haven*—working for someone else. Entrepreneurs, like CEOs of large companies, are shackled by an extraordinary range of obligations to employees, customers, and family. Unlike the CEO of a Fortune 500 company, we work under the restraints of fewer people, less money, and scant resources. Often limited knowledge or experience creates great worries for us. These worries are often faced alone. We may struggle with loneliness, long work days, and juggling to strike a balance between business and personal life. Too frequently, isolation may become the enemy. When stress kicks in—the fun stops.

This brings me to the writing of this book. I am a business coach and mentor specializing in business and personal growth and transformation. Over the past 20 years, I have worked with energetic and dedicated leaders who have an impressive range of intelligence and street smarts. What they share is a common desire for unlimited accomplishments. They also want more time and a quicker, less stressful path to success. Yet few tell me they can claim to have achieved this balance.

It is possible. I know this personally and from teaching thousands of business leaders and entrepreneurs how to have greater success while experiencing more freedom. I have written about these practices in this book so that you too can have what others have learned and implemented. My knowledge and experience from coaching, as well as a hands-on founder and CEO of my own companies, form the basis for the stories in this book.

Whether you are a seasoned entrepreneur with a growing company, a middle-stage business owner, or just starting up, this book will help you with distinctive challenges that entrepreneurs face:

Deal with your fears
Remain innovative
Cope with loneliness
Confront overwhelming *busy-ness*
Discover the meaning of success
Climb up from despair
Know yourself

Deal with your fears. Let's face it. We all have fears. The difference is that entrepreneurs have put themselves in the situation to have to face their fears more often than the average employee.

Fears can be in the areas of public speaking or networking to develop new business at an event. For others, the greatest fear might be firing an angry (perhaps unbalanced) employee. Many have panicked over not spending enough time with their children—with the concern that they'll look back in time and realize what they missed. Other fears? What about the fear of poor health and running yourself to the edge? Or the big fear that you could fail?

Remain innovative. Many entrepreneurs audaciously admit they're "in it for the money," yet when I question them further, they reveal that the challenge and creativity of building something from nothing makes the venture an irresistible addiction. Money is only a marker for their success. So then the question becomes: How do we keep that innovative spirit alive and unburdened?

Cope with loneliness. I've spoken with many entrepreneurs who actually feel like silent warriors. They depict themselves as headstrong fighters engaged in daily battle. The battlefield is strong with competition. Profit-and-loss (P&L) is the frontline measurement of their success, but daily solitary conflict takes its toll. Many don't talk about the weight of their concerns and frustrations, and this silence can lead to loneliness.

Confront overwhelming busy-ness. Many entrepreneurs tell me they barely have time to sleep, let alone take vacations or play. Men and women who have been running profitable companies for 20 years or more continue to feel the stress. They talk about sleepless nights, moments of bone-shaking anxiety, and personal doubt.

Discover the meaning of success. Successful leaders, as measured by their profits and losses, often don't feel successful. Even though they can read reports of their own progress, they admit they don't feel that they're *there* yet.

Climb up from despair. Yes, *despair* is a loaded word, but that's what leaders feel when they have a big dream that falls apart. Getting back up may be the hardest part of all.

Know yourself. It's not enough knowing *how to make your business grow.* At the heart of being an entrepreneur is the process of getting to know *yourself* better, including your unique capabilities and talents. Sure, you may compare yourself to others, who doesn't? You may be telling yourself that others are more educated, experienced, competitive, driven, personable, or business-minded. Maybe they are. But it's *your* distinct assets that can make you as successful as you want to be. Those assets are far more important than hard-driving competitiveness or an MBA when you're facing up to personal vulnerabilities, interpersonal challenges, and introspective reflections. So before you set out to *beat the competition*, or go back for your business degree, first, I want to help you rediscover your best friend—you. We'll do that, together, here, in this book.

I realize, of course, that every entrepreneur is different. Our motivations, personalities, backgrounds, and experiences are unique. Most of us share a drive for contribution, wealth, independence, and achievement, but these common goals arise from a wide range of deeper personal motivations.

In this book, I'll describe a lot of entrepreneurs who have met common challenges in highly individualistic ways. Reading about them, you're likely to recognize the rough and darker times that made them pause. And because I've coached others through these times, and have lived through them myself, I'll show you not only how to manage stress, frustration, disappointment, and negative emotions, but also how to get back your self-confidence, vitality, joy, and self-fulfillment for the choice you've made—that of being a successful entrepreneur, even when you don't think it's possible.

There are parts of this book that may seem like soft skills, maybe even *airy-fairy* stuff. But they're not. They are skills and techniques that have been used and mastered by some of the most successful people in history. Meditation is one of them, for instance. Yoga or Tai Chi is another. Spending time identifying your values is another. I believe these are among the most critical skills of all, for a very simple reason; we're all human.

Many entrepreneurs are so busy trying to do their business better, that they forget to put attention on the human side of things. Yet when these human skills are addressed—so that they improve the way they think, relate, communicate, listen, and hold their goals—they grow. And when they grow, their business automatically, almost miraculously, grows too. Growth from these soft skills may begin to happen so fast and easy that the business owner may begin to wonder if it wasn't there all the time to utilize. Perhaps it is these softer, more human skill sets that actually hold the ultimate answers for the fulfillment of balance in business and in life. Because when you're energized, happy, and self-confident, you have freedom to vibrantly and courageously lead your business forward and live your life out loud—with passion and purpose.

HONORING YOU, THE ENTREPRENEUR

Namaste is one of those words that when I say it, I feel internal peace. It's Sanskrit and means the light in me honors the light in you. And so from one entrepreneur to another,

Namaste.

| **1** | |

Take Out the Trash

When I let go of what I am, I become what I might be.

Lao Tzu

Katherine is a busy entrepreneur.

Here's what's going through her head on a typical day.

One moment she's exhilarated by the large deal that just closed. The next moment she's scratching her head, wondering how a good customer was lost to her competition.

Last month's numbers were in the black, this month they're in the red. She worries: is this going to be a trend? Denying that it will be, she pushes forward, ignoring the invisible worry-weight just added to her load.

With sales down, she must find a way to pay out bonuses from last quarter.

She's been researching better benefits, but now she's unsure about moving on it. Better wait until sales pick up.

Then, suddenly, good news—she hears from an account she's been pursuing for years: they're ready to make a deal. With that business come additional concerns. Now she has to support that sale. Does she need to hire additional employees? Where will she find them—quickly?

She opens up the mail. Her leased office space just increased.

The general manager walks into her office and states that the company can't hold off anymore in replacing some of the systems. Computers, printers, and the phones must be updated. She also reminds Katherine that the lease is up in two years—now is the time to reconsider relocating.

One of Katherine's managers confirms that a long-time employee must be fired. He has many peers in the company. How will the team take this news? She's worried about repercussions. Will they be distracted from their work and slow down business even more?

If just one of these issues alone weren't enough, a bomb is dropped on her. The company's star salesperson quits—to start his own company.

TRASH BUILD-UP

If you're an entrepreneur, you're probably nodding your head, and wincing, right now. It's likely that at times Katherine's problems parallel your problems. The tough decisions she has to make are similar. Facing mind-boggling dilemmas every day can leave you conflicted, exhausted, drained, and depleted of alternatives. Perhaps you've wondered secretly at times why you ever got into this business to begin with.

I, too, have been down this path and know the terrain quite well. I also know that it doesn't have to be this way. Stress and tension don't have to be key ingredients that go along with being an entrepreneur. There is a better path. This one can make those difficult, even gut-wrenching business decisions and issues more manageable. Granted, that may sound impossible. But I promise if you follow this, you will find yourself with less angst and more time for the things you love to do. It is all about taking out the trash.

Taking Out the Trash

Taking out the trash does not mean emptying the trashcan in the kitchen. The trash I'm talking about is insidious and it lies inside of you—deep inside your mind. This trash is created from past experiences. Some call them files or archives. They are momentary impressions left on your brain from an experience, whether positive or negative. They pop up out of the blue when you relate a current experience or feeling to a memory of something that happened in the past.

Think of walking into a bakery. The ovens baking breads and cakes give off aromas that delight the senses and a warmth the seems to envelop you, like comforting arms. Perhaps this experience kicks off a fond memory of going into a bakery with your mother when you were younger because she wanted to buy you a cookie or a cupcake for getting an A on a test.

Or you may have fallen down the steps when you were a child and now get anxious when you walk down a narrow staircase. Perhaps years ago you got pulled under by a wave in the ocean and almost drowned. Now when you're near the ocean, you get feelings of intense panic.

Trash is the pile up of unwanted, not useful connections to past experiences. It may stop someone from becoming unbelievably successful in his career because he his third grade teacher ridiculed him in front of the class when he forgot his homework. Another person may have a fear of public speaking which dates back to the time she stuttered and was made fun of.

Fears brew in trash. Something painful from the past controls your thinking and actions today. It is what blocks you from controlling your destiny, taking risks, or how much money or success you eventually achieve.

Just as trash can mess with keeping a positive state of mind, it can also cause the clutter of unnecessary thoughts that create stress and get in the way of running your business. In order to move your business toward the vision you have for it, you need clarity, something that trash thwarts. It's never easy to see your own trash, so I'll use Katherine and her business as our guide.

Katherine's Trash

At the age of 10, Katherine built a profitable street corner lemonade stand whose location, chosen carefully, was a busy neighborhood intersection. After a couple of years, she grew tired of this junior start-up that earned her a profit of $12 a week. She bestowed her business to a neighborhood boy who carried it on in her tradition.

Later, Katherine worked through high school for a series of entrepreneurs. Word processing and other low-paying office grunt work became her training ground. The work was boring, but the payoff was great—she had direct contact with the owners of the various companies she worked for. Her curiosity of business ownership was tweaked. It was early on that she looked forward to the day she'd build a business of her own.

Katherine found the opportunity to do just that. After graduating college, she took over managing a coffee shop, and then purchased it with a pay out over time to the owner. She was only 21 when she became a business owner. Acquiring her first shop led to opening another shop, then another. Within a few years she had nine stores. Quick success came from her innate ability to serve quality products in a comfortable atmosphere at a fair price. When she sold the business, Katherine made a strong return on her initial investment.

As she turned 26, she was already underway in her next business—a coffee and sandwich shop, serving only breakfast and lunch. Each month was a new theme featuring hot and cold drinks and sandwiches from around the world. She was on her way to repeating success by building another flourishing company.

Fred, another entrepreneur frequented the coffee shops and watched Katherine grow her business. He witnessed her strong work ethic and endless drive to succeed. Fred was starting up a customer care call center for the health-care industry. He wanted someone like Katherine to join him as an equal partner and to manage sales, employees, and customer service. Fred's strength was in operations—the backroom part of business. He presented Katherine with the offer to join him. At first, she dismissed the offer, knowing she wasn't ready to sell this business so soon. Also, she didn't have any experience in a call center. However, after many more convincing conversations with Fred, Katherine began to admire him. He'd certainly complement her skill set. He let her take the time she requested to mull over his offer, and at the end, came to a decision to move forward and join Fred in his venture. She put her new business up for sale and it sold quickly. Fred became her first partner in business.

As time went by, Katherine got married and started a family. Three years into the start up of the call center, Fred had a sudden heart attack and died. He was 62. Grief struck all those who loved him, but Katherine went into a state of shock.

On top of this unexpected loss of her good friend and business partner, Katherine now had the sole responsibility of running the company. She knew the front end part of the business—sales, employee relations, and customer service, but she had limited knowledge of the operations management of a call center. This brought her great doubt about how to move forward.

Doubt Is Trash

Doubt is deadly. It halts creativity and growth. Doubt is the mind playing tricks on you, slowing down movement and progress toward your goals. Doubt is trash building up. It creates confusion and roadblocks for the results you want. It fuels negativity. For Katherine, doubt and all its trickster thoughts kept flashing one vital question in front of her. Can I run the company by myself, without Fred?

Trash Collection

Katherine always had doubts about herself, who doesn't? But she kept them hidden well. It wasn't until after Fred's death that these doubt gremlins showed up in full gear.

Katherine was able to keep her doubt-trash in the background, trying to not let it interfere with what she needed to do. By the time she turned 34, she was running a $10 million company that employed 25 people. She was hungry to expand, and even though she had built the company successfully to this point, she didn't have the confidence or experience to build it any further by herself.

Since her relationship with Fred had been a synergistic one, she was left with positive feelings about partnerships. She would bring in people with expertise in areas where she was weakest, then offer these people shares in the company.

Her trash was silent, and she ignored it, as it was revving up to make mischief.

New Partners, More Trash

After a long and thorough search, John, Howard, and Susan became Katherine's new partnership team.

John was a 40-year-old investor who came from a publicly traded pharmaceutical firm. Laid off during a downsizing, he decided not to retreat back into the financial department of another behemoth organization. Instead, he ventured out on his own as a financial investor. He soon discovered that working for someone else and earning a weekly income was much different than hunting for your own food. Katherine and John were introduced to each other by a headhunter. The two clicked immediately, and his strong financial background proved to be a good complement to Katherine's managerial skills.

Howard, a retired attorney, worked in health care. At 50, he came into an inheritance from his uncle who didn't have any children of his own. He became a millionaire overnight. The first thing he did, as is the fantasy of most people who come into a fortune, was to quit his job. But after a year of traveling with his wife, a retired school teacher, he had grown tired of all play and no work. He missed the business world. He was a good fit for Katherine's company.

Katherine needed a sales manager. Enter Susan, a 29-year-old, single, MBA graduate from an Ivy League university. Susan had moved up the ladder from sales rep to sales manager in a bio-tech organization. She moved on to become vice president of a start-up company in the same industry. Katherine pursued Susan hard, won her over, and brought her onboard as sale manager and her third partner.

Katherine's team was in place.

But . . .

Out of the four partners, Katherine was the only one with business ownership knowledge and experience. Her partners excelled in investing, legal issues, or sales, and knew little about visionary leadership from the top. None of them had ever owned a business of this size. Even John, who had a financial background and understood profit and loss, had never managed a company this complex.

As the business grew, so did the complications. Extra personnel were hired, additional procedures implemented, and of course, more sales were needed to feed the cash-hungry demands of a growing organization.

Katherine imagined that bringing in partners would simplify her life—instead, many things became more complicated. With four partners, the playing-field boundaries grew tighter. Katherine complained that her hands were tied. Decisions she had made so readily in the past were now more difficult. She had hoped that consensus decisions could be made by all the partners. Instead, she found they rarely agreed with each other.

All the partner issues, Katherine discovered, became her sole responsibility. But that didn't lessen her other obligations. She was still ultimately accountable for meeting sales objectives and driving the vision. She tried to find time in the evening to network and do some business development and still be home to put her children to bed. With so much to do, Katherine rarely sat still long enough to contemplate what was happening or to delve more deeply into her thoughts.

Katherine grew unhappy in her role. Often exhausted, she didn't realize that for the first time in her career, she was seeing the glass half empty. Solutions seemed far-off, possibly unreachable.

As stress crept in, taking advantage of this crack in the leadership foundation, Katherine noticed that she was losing her leadership power. She still headed up the company, but she greatly felt the loss of energy and confidence. The aura of her personal power had originally inspired others and enabled Katherine to grow the company, but now it was growing dim.

ANOTHER WAY

In rough outline, this was Katherine's situation when we first talked. I'd seen this before with other clients. As problems mount, the stakes become higher and the list of people depending on you, becomes greater. The toll of stress goes off the charts. Challenges look like unsolvable mysteries instead of intriguing puzzles. The quirks of the people who work for you—such as the things about them that used to make you laugh—begin to look like fatal flaws that, left unchecked, could sink the whole operation. Meanwhile, your to-do lists get longer while the performance expectations you place on your managers, your team, and yourself grow more unreasonable. Decision-making is reduced to the time it takes to have morning coffee; then the time it takes to walk down the hall; and, finally, the time it takes to answer the phone or tap out a gut response on a Blackberry. The worst is, what used to be fun, isn't fun anymore.

Where could Katherine go, given her tangled web of responsibilities, ambitions, and anxieties?

Before she and I could work out the answer, we had to begin with something very fundamental; her thinking and the buildup of trash.

The Limits of Working Harder

Like Katherine, if we're not getting the results we want, we often end up putting in longer hours and working harder. Working harder is usually not the long term answer. If we can recognize that our thinking is the foundation for whatever situation we face, we gain control. With control, comes an opportunity for change. This gives us access to more options and solutions and leads us to the results we want. In the end, what's required is not more effort, but less. But before you can take this counterintuitive step—achieving more by doing less—you'll have to explore your mindset. Stronger results with a centered, calmer, and focused mind come when the leadership practice of *thinking* is explored and the trash is taken out.

When the days are as busy as an entrepreneur's, who has the time to stop and explore their thinking or take out the trash? And even if you did have time, do you put thinking at the top of your list? Most people don't.

Thinking is not the same as processing data or absorbing information. The weather person on TV gives you the temperature and then suggests how to dress for the day. That is data. Fashion magazines show the newest styles for the season—the clothes you can't be without. Good information. And so it goes. Thinking about how to solve a problem from a different viewpoint takes time and work, perhaps more than we want to spend in an already time limited day. Thinking outside of the box is valuable because it brings alternative solutions to recurring unresolved issues which can increase productivity, creativity, and profitability, the time restraints we face, and the challenges to constantly produce quickly. However, people in business often confide in me that they just don't have the time to stop and do more in-depth thinking.

And if they did, they wouldn't even know where to begin. This is where I'll challenge my clients, like Katherine, because it is the depth of your thinking that differentiates the leaders from the followers. True *thinkers* make strong leaders.

Accomplished leaders understand that everything they do begins with their state of mind. Getting consciously connected to your thoughts will give more of the desired results you want, leading to a feeling of internal peace.

That seems pretty abstract. But consider Katherine's situation. What would it mean if she became a more intentional thinker? How would it make a difference in her daily life? How would it help her problems be less onerous and her rewards more fulfilling? How would it help her to remove the trash build-up?

PARTNERSHIP

With Katherine's three current partners, nothing could be accomplished without a battle. Negotiating with them had become a constant chore. Katherine often felt drained before the day even began.

She worked hard to train her partners to run a company this size and to help her grow it. She spent hours each week with them, meeting as a group or one-on-one, educating them about everything from managing people to profit and loss and operations. But their naiveté and stubbornness over expansion costs appeared as petty arguments. She wondered why she hadn't seen this before she brought them on board. After all, they knew about her desire to expand the company from the first moment they spoke—that was to be their purpose. Initially, she had been excited by the prospect of fielding such an excellent team. Now she reconsidered.

With disillusion came doubt. Not only did Katherine doubt her partners, but also herself. How could she have not seen this coming? How in the world could she have thought this partnership would be good? In the past, she considered herself an optimist with great insight. Now her thoughts were inclined to be pessimistic. She spoke about the narrow vision of her partners. Sadly, she felt as though her own vision, too, had been narrowed by all the conflicts that needed to be resolved.

A lot of precious hours—time that should have been spent growing the company—was instead directed to addressing problems in the partnership. So Katherine's challenge wasn't just partner-management or time-management. Her challenge was the buildup of doubt, mistrust, and embittered conflict—all indications of the clutter of trash that blocks the path to success. If she was to find her way out of this, there was only one thing to do: change her *thinking*, shifting it to an entirely different level. All these partnership problems aside, what was her ultimate *vision* of where this company—her company—was going? How could she keep this vision alive, exciting, and ever-present at the forefront of her thinking while managing partner issues?

As Katherine and I continued to discuss and process the challenges she faced alongside her vision, and shift her mindset from doubt to excitement and hope, she began to shift—to open up to other possibilities she had never seen or imagined. She realized it was her—and her thinking—that was clogging up their corporate system. The partnership issues were just a symptom of this. With that insight, she now had access to recreate her partnership and her company.

Declaration Statements: Howard

Katherine realized she would have to dump out old thoughts about her partners. This did not mean dumping her partners. It was her thinking *about* them that had to go in the trash. We created an exercise where she wrote down a simple statement that declared the greatest strength of each partner. Those statements would become her mantra during trying times.

For instance, she began to see Howard as already retired. He didn't seem to put in the hours that everyone else put in. He was slower in movements and getting things accomplished. There was no urgency to do anything. So Katherine wrote a declaration statement that declared Howard's greatest strength. He had a great relationship with the employees. He took the time to really listen and be with them. Her statement for Howard was this:

> Howard is the key to employee loyalty and retention.

Although he worked slower, she couldn't change that. But where he brought value was immeasurable. Good employee retention and strong loyalty would save the company much money if turnover remained low.

Declaration Statements: John

John had cut his teeth in corporate America. Instead of what *couldn't be done*, John's motto was *anything's possible*. When he jumped ship to join Katherine, he had little sales knowledge and was unsure of how to talk about the company's services to prospects. Doubting his ability to sell, John had a big trashcan to empty if he were to fit well into a blossoming entrepreneurial enterprise. He did, however, have a great knowledge of finances and could find a way to make, what seemed financially impossible, happen. His magic was with numbers. This was invaluable to Katherine. Her declaration statement for John was this:

> John is a true entrepreneur, knowledgeable, and able to make things happen.

Declaration Statements: Susan

Susan was born with a silver spoon in her mouth. She grew up in Boston, attended private schools, and then Ivy League colleges. She earned an MBA, moved out into the workforce and started her journey moving up the ranks of Fortune 500 companies. She had a chip on her shoulder, though, that broadcast her opinion that she was better than others. As annoying as this was, Katherine knew that Susan could sell like no one else she had ever seen. She was willing to put up with Susan's airs if she could bring in the revenues needed. Her declaration for Susan was this:

> Susan is a superstar at building sales leaders and generating revenue.

Initially, these declaration statements were a stretch. But Katherine trained herself to focus on her new thinking—the declaration statements about each of these partners. And as that happened, a very interesting transformation took place. The partnership shifted. They all began to connect. She was creating a new reality. And it all began from a shift in her thinking. She didn't have to push or strain to get people to change. She didn't have to continue restless nights of sleep worrying about what to say to train her partners to think about expansion. They were contributing to the expansion in more subtle, unexpected, yet tremendously valuable ways. But first she had to see this. If she continued down the trash-ridden path of negativity, she would have never noticed them in this new light. Her energy and enthusiasm returned. She reconnected to her positive personal power. Before long, that transformation was reflected in her company's performance. Within several months, the company's growth took off. Katherine felt that, once again, her business was on the road to expansion. Best of all, she started having fun again.

A new foundation had been developed upon which to build partner relationships. It didn't come from pushing harder, working longer, or worry. It didn't come from dumping old partners and replacing them with new ones. It came from a complete, intentional, decisive change in thinking—starting with hers.

Back to Taking Out the Trash

Of course, Katherine's shift in thinking did not happen overnight. It began where I think the process needs to begin for any entrepreneur . . . with the step that's the title of this chapter. With *taking out the trash*.

But let me explain why I've chose to start this book with taking out the trash.

The trash I'm talking about is something we all have. It's not the stuff that piles up with candy wrappers, paper, or junk mail in that black plastic receptacle under your desk. This trash is more destructive in nature. It takes up residence inside of you. It's in your mind, weaving doubt and negativity, moment by moment, as you go about your business (or try to!).

In a normal day you'll plan, prepare, worry, and think. Many times, all these interconnected mental processes are tied up in your own concerns and also your regard for others—employees, friends, and family. Some days the trash is at a minimum; other days it's overflowing. But whatever the level, it needs to *go*. When the trash is taken out, your energy is higher, your passion shows, and you're better able to make decisions that not only support your inner sense of well-being, but also the long-term interests of your company.

Most entrepreneurs are up to something big—all of the time. By something big, I mean they want more. Maybe more looks like more revenue or a higher profit margin. Or maybe more is greater market awareness, good customers, or hiring cream-of-the-crop employees to lead your company forward. Then, just when you're on to something big—*BAM*, suddenly you're off course. It happens all the time. It's a law of nature. It's as if the universe is testing you. Questioning you with, "Do you really want this?" "How far are you willing to go to get it?"

These tests make you hesitate and reconsider. Should you be going for this goal? Doubts get woven-in to your thoughts. The negativity creates a revolution inside you. This trash builds up, becoming a roadblock. But what is that roadblock really? It's nothing more than a collection of thoughts that need to go.

And we all have trash.

It's what keeps us from thinking clearly. It usurps our valuable time and energy, taking us away from the tasks at hand. Our patience wears thin. We begin over-reacting to situations that we normally handled well. We may second-guess ourselves, rehashing decisions we've already made. This trash, this clutter, becomes a distraction in our day, our business, our leadership, and our lives.

A strong leader must be sure that his or her mind is freed up and clear. The vision is paramount—not the trash. But when you face days that are one rollercoaster ride after another, how can you clear your mind to make confident decisions?

A FRESH START IN YOUR THINKING PROCESS

There are four most important questions to ask yourself to help keep your thinking clear. There are four daily practices that will help you remain centered even during the roughest days. Here, in summary, are the questions to which you need answers—and the practices that help you move decisively toward clearer thinking.

ASK YOURSELF

Take some quality time to get quiet, close your eyes, and ask yourself these questions.

1. What can I do each day to become more aware of my thinking and to keep my mind clear?
2. Do I feel boxed in, knowing there are solutions out there, though I'm not able to get at them?
3. Who am I blaming for my problems?
4. Am I aware of my statements that begin with the deadly: should-have, could-have, or would-have?

PRACTICE THIS

Now you're ready to move into daily practices that will help you to get free from self-imposed limitations.

Practice #1: Use This 5,000 Year Old Business Tool

There is an age-old practice that has been used by millions of people to improve self-awareness, help solve problems, promote a deep sense of inner peace, reduce stress, slow down aging, and enhance health. That practice is called *meditation*. If you're thinking shaved heads, long-flowing garments, and chanting—think again. This is not *woo-woo* stuff. Instead, think—everyday business people dressed in business attire. These are the new students of meditation. Meditation is coming out of the closet and finding a new home in the business world. Meditation helps leaders make wiser decisions, communicate with more depth and sincerity, listen more intently, be more confident, and lead with greater strength and conviction—and hallelujah, less ego. It's a very powerful, yet simple method for creating awareness, establishing a sense of balance, and grounding your thoughts.

Meditation involves getting quiet—something we can all do. But because it may be a newly introduced tool, it will take some practice. As you get quiet and turn your attention from the outer world to your inner world, you'll reach a higher state of consciousness. In this state, you'll see solutions to problems you never saw before.

To smoothly transition from your hectic day to meditation, begin with this grounding exercise that I use. Find a quiet place and sit in a chair with your spine straight. If you prefer, you can sit on the floor with your legs crossed. Close your eyes and take some deep, cleansing breaths. Imagine a soft light enveloping you, protecting your personal space. Feel the warmth of the light around you and the strength of the ground beneath you. As you breathe, imagine throwing out any trash you've collected. Toss out insecurities, doubt, anger, fear, and blame. You don't have to name each negative thought as you're letting it go, instead you may just want to do a collective trash heave.

Now that you've moved into a quieter state, take some deeper breaths—focusing only on your breathing. Breathe in through your nose for four counts and breathe out through your mouth for eight counts. Keep breathing just like that and imagine, with each inhalation, you are taking in positive energy. And as you exhale, imagine you are letting go of stress, negativity, and fear.

Allow any thoughts that enter your mind to just pass through and exit immediately. More will enter and exit—let them. Don't try to stop them—you can't. Don't let them stay. Just let them go and don't hold on to any of them. This exercise should be effortless. No pushing, trying, or stress is involved. It is a gentle releasing of the flow of incessant thoughts. As soon as you release one, automatically a sly perpetrator might sneak back in, unnoticed at first. However, because you are doing this meditation practice, you'll begin to notice thoughts that come and go and others that want to stick around. Your only task here is to keep releasing them. Out in the real world, during your busy day, these collective thoughts aren't released. They take hold, find a home inside, and begin to gnaw away at your inner peace, clouding up your thinking. Creating havoc on your mental health and eventually showing up as a pain or illness in your body. The more you practice releasing thoughts during meditation, the more you'll learn to seduce them into silence in the real world also. Giving yourself a good dose of natural medication costs nothing and has only positive results.

Practice meditating as long as you can in one sitting. Start slowly at first. Maybe two minutes once a day. Then, at each sitting, add more minutes. Try to build up to 15 minutes twice a day. I like to meditate first thing in the morning after I brush my teeth and before I work out. It helps me start my day with a clearer mind. To end my day, before I get into bed I meditate again, sitting in a chair and letting go of all the thoughts that have accumulated during an active day. This soothes me into a more peaceful sleep. As you quiet your mind, you're taking out the trash—those disruptive, self-defeating thoughts. And as you take out the trash, you gain greater control over stress and fear-based thoughts. You're better able to see the obstacles in your path and maneuver around them more easily.

When I've had a difficult day, I may put on some headphones and listen to a CD by Kelly Howell, the founder of Brain Sync. She uses sound waves to alter the brain state for more relaxation, creativity, health, and well being. If her calming voice doesn't soothe your mind, the music certainly will.

Whether you're a novice or quite experienced at meditating, it is a continual practice. There is nothing to perfect or get better at. It's just a matter of being able to sit still, quietly, and do absolutely nothing but breathe and empty your mind.

Although meditation is one of those easy-to-do, easy-to-use, nothing-to-buy remedies, it will take great discipline in the beginning. You'll make excuses not to do it. Do it anyway. You're too busy? Do it anyway. Too tired? Do it anyway. Pressed for time? Do it anyway.

All entrepreneurs want ways to measure success in anything they do. You'll know success in your meditation practice by the level of peace you feel within, by revitalized energy, and increased focus. I suppose that's why it has been practiced for over 5,000 years.

Practice #2: Let Go!

Recently I was speaking to a lawyer who heads up his own law firm. He and his partners were having lots of breakdowns in their communication. They couldn't agree on anything, so nothing could get done. He'd try to push his partners to make decisions—any decisions at this point would be good, he said. It seemed the harder he pushed them to agree to take some actions, the further they were pushed away from doing just that. Some days he wanted to punch the walls from frustration, he told me. Other times, he said, he'd sit at his desk and stare at the walls as if waiting it out for something to change.

When we want something badly and it is not happening, the tendency is to work harder to get it. Perhaps if we really press hard, we'll get the result we want from sheer persistence. But that's like pushing out a baby before it's ready to be born. It can't happen. Pushing harder isn't the answer. If you keep pounding at the problem, believing the answer will come, you're likely to get nowhere and all you'll have is one big headache.

Why not reverse the process and release your need to push to get something or be somewhere? Begin by letting go of what you really want, hard as that may be to do. You'll have to use some trust in this practice—trust that letting go, instead of pushing or trying hard, will bring you closer to what you want. Letting go is letting something be as it is. When you can let go of those thoughts of *it must happen or else*, you'll automatically gain easier access to getting it—as if all along, it was right under your nose and you couldn't see it because you were too busy thinking it had to be attained in a certain way. When you lighten up your grip on a problem, the answers have room to flow in. The harder you hold on and push for it to happen, the more that problem will get a grip on you, instead of you getting a hold of what you want.

Several years ago, I attended a weekend seminar on behavioral change with a group of 300 people. The audience struggled with the speaker's question: "How do you get from Point A (your current difficult problem) to Point B (the solution)?" When no one seemed to answer to her satisfaction, she grew quiet. In the ensuing silence, this petite woman bellowed out, pronouncing each letter as if it were its own word: "L-E-T G-O!"

She wanted to shatter the tight hold we have on how something must be achieved. How we envision something happening can be a very limiting thought or belief. And we also make it much harder to get. Our limiting beliefs become our current way of thinking and we stay stuck. Then we push harder and harder, get stressed, frustrated, and confused, as we block out an alternative solution—the right solution.

As you let go of old beliefs, you'll make room for new ones that work better for you today. To get what you want and become what you want, you must take those old thoughts and—L-E-T G-O!

Try this. When you find yourself churning away at problems, staring blankly at walls, or self-absorbed in thought—stop. Stop whatever you're doing. If you're driving, pull off to the side of the road. Take some deep breaths. The oxygen you breathe in will relax you. Oxygen is a natural relaxant.

It has no side effects and is free. Relax your body—your neck, your shoulders, your face, making your way down to your toes. Now focus on the present moment. Stop thinking about what needs to be done. As you bring yourself into the present moment, you'll release frustration and old beliefs and clear your mind to allow for new and better solutions. You'll be letting go of trash.

Practice #3: Rid Yourself of Your Response to Blame

I remember a *Three Stooges* episode where someone yelled at them, "Who did this?"

They were always getting in trouble. Larry, Moe, and Curly responded by each simultaneously pointing to the other. Although the audience always got a laugh from that action, it represents how many people don't want to own the responsibility for something they did wrong. It pronounces, "I'm not taking any ownership for this."

If you've made a mistake and someone accuses you or blames you for it, don't say, "I don't know how this happened." What you're then indicating is *I was asleep at the wheel and I don't want to admit it.*

Some blame others.

"We got the wrong information, so it's not our fault, it's theirs," or "That's her responsibility, not mine."

And then there's the turn-around blame, taking someone off guard. Someone blames you and you blame them right back. "I don't see what you're so upset about, you're making too much of a big deal out of nothing."

Getting blamed for a mistake or not doing a good enough job, never feels good. But making excuses for what happened will only make you feel worse because you've taken away any control. Now you become a victim. In addition, there is no learning that can happen when you're a victim because you are dodging what you did. And growth and progress are stunted. Strong leaders own their mistakes. They don't take on a victim's roll of making up excuses.

Blame retards growth and stifles positive energy, so when you hear it coming out of your mouth, stop. Remove it from your thoughts. Instead, own what happened, as in "I made a mistake."

We're all human beings prone to making mistakes. Sometimes the mistakes are huge. The beauty of a making a mistake is that we can learn and grow from it. You have the opportunity to do it differently next time.

Practice #4: Watch Your Should-haves, Could-haves, and Would-haves

Should-haves are toxic to entrepreneurs. They destroy enthusiasm, motivation, and joy. They create guilt and fear, blocking your ability to think clearly. I have heard so many entrepreneurs tell me, I *should have* done it differently. Or, if only I *could have* known, I *would have* gotten that deal.

I've never known business leaders who could go back in time and change the mistakes they've made. What's done is done. There is nothing you can do to change the past.

But there is something you can do to change your thoughts. Take out the trash. Should-haves cloud your reality in the present moment because they keep your thoughts in the past. When you're wondering about what could have happened in the past, you take yourself out of the present moment. Being purely in the moment brings no worries. If you are just *being here now* there is no need to feel badly. Being in the present is what brings us happiness. Try hiking a mountain or reading a book. You're so purely and effortlessly in the moment. Happy, aren't you?

Should-haves chip away at your energy level and enthusiasm and gradually erodes your personal power—your source of confidence. When your thoughts are in should-have, could-have, and would-have mode, you doubt yourself. You hold back on taking risks because maybe you'll make the same mistake again. Then what will others think?

To take out the trash, drop should-have, could-have, and would-have from your thoughts and vocabulary.

Here's how to do that. Next time you hear yourself say, "I *should have*"— just stop!

Next, let's replace the should-have talk with a question. Ask yourself, what can I do now? Keep asking that question. This will bring you into being in the present moment, and put you on track for forward movement, instead of keeping you stuck in the past. You'll take your thoughts off of what didn't happen and focus on what you can do to make things happen. Possibility abounds.

SUMMARY

☑ You can free yourself from self-imposed limitations, or the trash build up in your mind, which hinders growth, progress, and self-confidence.

☑ Meditation is a very powerful, yet simple method for creating awareness, establishing a sense of balance, grounding your thoughts in the present moment, and clearing your mind.

☑ Meditation will help you to relax, become more focused, and open you up to alternative solutions.

☑ You can meditate at any time, in any place.

☑ When you reframe your thoughts, results for your business will also change.

☑ Let go of what you can't control.

☑ Use declaration statements to shift your thinking.

☑ When blamed for something you've done wrong, own it and take accountability. Learn from your mistakes and grow.

☑ Stop negative self talk.

☑ Take should-have, would-have, and could-have out of your vocabulary. They will disempower you. The past is done. Move on with more energy and clarity.

2

Go Ahead—Be Different!

Today you are You, that is truer than true. There is no one alive who is Youer than You.

Happy Birthday to You, Dr. Seuss

Inauthenticity is a saboteur—a silent killer of motivation, personal power, and life force. Just ask Andrew.

As an entrepreneur who desperately wanted to succeed, he had started several companies, one after the other. His more recent one, a nutrition and diet services business, gave him insight into the destructive force of inauthenticity.

Never quite satisfied with himself, Andrew sought to be a better leader. He tried emulating other greats, such as Winston Churchill, Martin Luther King, and Mahatma Gandhi—reading and observing how they communicated and lead. His method didn't work; instead of incorporating elements of these impressive leaders into his personal style, he tried to replace his own style entirely. Unwilling to accept himself as he was, unable to find a leadership style that was his match, and failing to be like those he admired, led to greater discontent.

It was on the eve of yet another failed business that his world turned upside down, as if the universe was whispering, "Wake up. Become yourself. It's the only person you can truly be."

Was it too late for Andrew?

ANDREW'S STORY: ON HIS OWN

After 20 years of working his way up the corporate ladder in a food manu-facturing company, Andrew finally became a vice president. A few years later, after his promotion, he grew weary of the cold mid-western winters. He felt restless during those wintry months and suffered from one sinus infection after another. Although he traveled overseas for weeks at a time, he dreaded returning to the bitter cold at home.

When his company began volunteer layoffs, Andrew made the difficult decision to take a termination package. He could make the warmer southeast his new home. Despite 12 months of pay and benefits in his layoff package, Andrew was determined to complete his job search in six months. This would allow another six months of passive income that could be invested, then applied toward college education for his twin pre-teen daughters.

Becoming Self-Employed

Sara, his childhood sweetheart and wife of 17 years had confidence in his ability to find a comparable paying job in the south. She too wanted to leave the long, cold winter months.

Andrew and Sara sold their house within three months and relocated south. They found the home of their dreams, three miles from the beach, in a school district that got high ratings. After six months of a job search, Andrew was frustrated. He was overqualified for the types of positions he was interviewing for. Several colleagues tried to convince him to go out on his own. He knew the food industry well and was a good operations manager, although he lacked strong people skills. If he started his own business, his ability with numbers, strategy, and organization could help compensate for his weaker skills. Hiring a sales person would be important so he could focus on the back end of business.

Andrew and Sara developed a financial plan to explore the viability of starting up a company. It could be done. With help from the U.S. Small Business Administration, Andrew put together a business plan, talked to his lawyer to set up a legal entity, and established a line of credit with a bank. He was ready to open the doors to his own distribution business. His customers would be retail health food chains who had an online presence.

Andrew hired a sales person who quit two months later after claiming she wasn't earning enough.

Failure

Eleven months later, Andrew sadly closed the business, and with a fresh new image restarted it up under a different name. Not much else changed. Andrew's disappointment at this major failure took a chunk out of his already questionable self-esteem.

In this second business, Andrew would not rely on a salesperson to build it. He would use his network for business development. It didn't work. After eight months of struggle, he closed his second company. Andrew blamed it on his lack of knowledge in sales, the fierce competition, and his personal cash crunch. Disappointed again, but surprisingly still determined, Andrew was ready to try again, knowing this would be the last chance he'd get. If he couldn't make it with this third company, he'd have to go back to a job search and accept a lower responsibility position. Andrew had dipped into their children's college fund investment to get his companies financed, and he was clear that he wouldn't lose it all to his failures. The pressure was great.

Once again he examined past mistakes. It all came back to sales—without it, he knew he didn't have a company. As he researched different businesses, he found an avenue where he wouldn't have to sell belly to belly. He was going to market products online. The Internet would help do the selling for him.

Success finally came to Andrew. This new business grew slowly for the first two years—but he had made it further than ever before. He even began to replenish the borrowed college funds.

Still there was a familiar unease of failure looming around the corner. He couldn't put his finger on it. It felt like a noose tightening around his neck. It kept him up at night. Was he predicting his own doom?

THE PROBLEM

Andrew was an introvert. He also wasn't very confident. A painfully shy child, he had to push himself hard to be amongst other children. Lucky for him, he was blessed with athletic ability. But sometimes he never got to display those assets due to his near crippling problem. Because he was so quiet, other children couldn't figure him out and so they labeled him odd.

Unless the other kids he played ball with knew him, he was typically chosen last. Standing there alone as the other boys looked at him was just too agonizing.

As a teenager, his discomfort with other people did not go away. In high school, he tried hard to dismiss who he was. Andrew tried out for the school play. He threw his name into the hat as captain of the writing club. Making the decision to participate in both of these was much more painful than not making the cut.

As an adult, Andrew continued to challenge himself and worked hard on his insecurity. Still, when around successful people, he got awkwardly stiff, becoming self-conscious and critical of his inadequacies. At social functions, when others gathered together talking and laughing, he'd find an empty room, pull out his Blackberry, and check e-mail or write a to-do list—anything to avoid people.

Unrealistic Standards

Many of us, like Andrew, have painful childhood experiences that shape our adult future. If Andrew was to be successful, he would have to confront his low confidence level and introversion head-on. It would be the only way to diminish its power over him.

To do this, he studied biographies of famous leaders. From his studies, he tried to think like these people, talk like them, and behave like them. It didn't work. Although Andrew held high standards for running a business, his inauthenticity brought mistrust. He lost himself as he tried to be like someone else. People couldn't figure him out. He hid behind the images of those he studied.

Bill Gates, one of the people at the top of his list, has an incredible blend of brilliance, competitive drive, and purposeful insight. A technician turned entrepreneur with a combination of charisma and self-deprecation, and an uncanny ability to generate success and wealth, Andrew's skills dwarfed in the shadows of this billionaire. Yet Andrew tried to replicate Gate's style, just as he had with other leaders he admired, but couldn't pull it off. It just made him feel more awkward and out of place.

How does an entrepreneur, like Andrew, with the desire to build a successful company, and an internal dialog that highlights inferiority, break out?

Masking Authenticity

Andrew wanted to be a great business owner and also comfortable with his style of leadership. His desire to speak comfortably with people and to also empower himself is a gift he sought. Because he didn't like who he was, he hid behind a mask and couldn't show his true self to the world. Wanting to emulate others, then failing, he became confused and frustrated on just how to *be*. Sure Andrew is a nice guy, a loving family man, and a decent boss. But he failed to show up as the leader he *already* was. Who is the real Andrew? Where does he stand on issues? Can people count on him to be consistently himself? Until he becomes empowered by the leader he already is—an authentic leader who is true to himself—his ego, insecurities, and fears will continue to block both personal and business growth. Long lasting success cannot adhere to an inner core of inauthenticity.

Instead of doing him a service, the mask became a sneaky thief, robbing him of his true character and veiling reality. What kind of a leader would Andrew like to be? The kind he is not. Gregarious, humorous, and comfortable around people, his new self would be better at running a business and communicating with others—instead of the crippling leader he sees when he looks inward. The mask he wears creates a wall, keeping others on the outside. People can't figure him out. He's more comfortable with that. Because if they really knew who he was, they'd see what he sees—an inadequate leader. A fraud. His constant battle with what he should be and who he really is, gets shielded from the judging eyes of others.

Andrew was selling out. With no place to stand, no connection to his core values and purpose, he had become confused. Instead of relating to people from his heart, where genuine relationships can be built, he over analyzed everything—staying in his head—a dangerous place for anyone. Andrew had no idea that his perceived disagreeable parts of himself might endear him to others, instead of turning them away. Opposing forces were at work.

Wake Up!

Andrew's struggle with his own identity was reaching an all time low when the wake up call came. Almost two years into this third business, sales were down. He had lost a major buyer due to competition. Then an opportunity to close a large sale presented itself. A lot rode on this presentation.

Nothing had changed about Andrew to insure that this deal got closed. He continued to spend a lot of energy covering up who he was and little time developing himself.

The turning point for Andrew came from his next failure. His great ability to persevere even with all his handicaps would eventually bring him success, but he'd have to weather one more storm. The biggest one he faced so far.

Andrew had to make a presentation to a group of executive buyers for a large health food chain in the Northwest. He never performed well at presentations, but usually could muddle his way through. This one was different. The entire team of eight buyers was going to be present. His last presentation to four of these same buyers was about three years ago, when he botched it up. Though prepared with the product knowledge, his ability to connect with people did not leave them with a sense of trust. They instead selected to make this huge purchase from his competitor. Andrew went home sick that night. His head felt like it was splitting open and his stomach was tied up in knots. It took weeks for him to get over the humiliation and loss.

This time he did not want to repeat the past. Determined to win the deal, he brought a colleague along to do his talking. Jim and Andrew had been college roommates at Temple University. They had met in their freshman year when they both joined the same fraternity. Jim was a psychology major who was outgoing and didn't have to study much to get good grades. Andrew was a business major at the Fox School of Business, and studied most of his free time. They made good roommates and developed into close friends. Jim and Andrew stayed in touch after school, marriage, and children. Jim became a psychologist and took corporate positions in human resources. Later he got involved in sales, then sales training for a national organization.

The presentation was to be held in Chicago where Jim resided. When Andrew called upon Jim to step in for him and to give the presentation to the team of buyers, Jim didn't hesitate. Andrew prepared the PowerPoint slides and walked Jim through the product information. They were ready. While Jim presented, Andrew sat on the sidelines, not saying a word, hoping the four buyers from three years ago wouldn't remember him. Jim's presentation went well and Andrew knew they had bagged the deal. The executives seemed interested, except for one, Bill, who was new at the company and deemed an up and coming star. It was Bill who asked to speak to Andrew privately.

Leaving the room and before the door could close behind them, Bill open fired at Andrew. He reprimanded him for being the president of his company and not even having the courtesy to speak directly to the eight buyers. Bill wanted to hear about the company from Andrew. He wasn't looking for a sales pitch, but for a connection with the person who had the passion to build this company. He wanted to be sold on Andrew, then his company, and lastly the product. Andrew was mortified. His cheeks became like red apples and he could feel the perspiration building on his scalp. He was paralyzed. He couldn't move for fear of stumbling over his own feet. It seemed like hours before Bill quieted down—after disgracing him with his inability to be a good representative for his company. His parting remarks hit home. Bill found Andrew's actions rude and disrespectful. He didn't ask for an explanation and Andrew was certainly not in the right frame of mind to volunteer one.

He lost the deal. Again. Unbelievable as it could be to Andrew, the humiliation was greater than the last time. He wanted to dig a hole and bury himself in it. When Bill had finished his tirade, Andrew mumbled an apology, shook his hand, gathered up Jim, the PowerPoint presentation and any remnants of his persona, and flew home. On the plane, he kept replaying the day as he sunk deeper and deeper into despair. A week later, I met Andrew for the first time.

AUTHENTIC LEADERSHIP

Andrew charged his failures with the external environment—such as cash crunch and the economy. I questioned him on his competitors. He was confused that they were thriving. A good reality check. If Andrew's competitors were doing well while he was failing (again), the economy and his other excuses couldn't be given full blame for his situation

To build an enduring organization and gain employee and customer loyalty and trust, a leader must be authentic. These times demand it. We require a leader who shares his values and isn't afraid to stand by them. He must be two sided in his leadership—leading from both his head and his heart. Authenticity resides in the heart. Perhaps that is why this was Andrew's Achilles' heel. Good at analysis, planning, and organization, he never learned how to lead from his heart, where real connections with people get made. And trust and long-term relationships are solidified.

Andrew would be forced to make a choice in the near future. He could do some work on his mindset, transform and grow—or close another business. He had only one task in front of him if he was going to change—ironically it was to become the leader he already was.

The wake up call from the sales presentation fiasco created an opportunity. For many of us, like Andrew, it takes hitting rock bottom to wake us up. Maybe it's that hard hit on our heads as we land that jolts us to a higher level of consciousness, awakening us out of sleepwalking. Andrew's eyes were opening.

At the heart of being an entrepreneur is the opportunity of getting to know yourself better, including your unique capabilities and talents, and your inner voice—your guidance system. Andrew's desire to be like the leaders he admired, those glorified leaders portrayed in the media, as he disregarded his authenticity, would only bring continued failure. If he was going to turnaround his company, he'd have to change.

When Andrew discovered that he was the actual perpetrator of success, we were then able to set up steps for him to make changes. As Andrew's camouflage was peeled away, the authentic Andrew emerged.

Steps toward Change

> 1. First, he was tasked with the job of shedding his mask—coming to terms with his strengths and weaknesses.
> 2. Next, he would allow others to see them as he removed the mask.
> 3. Connecting to his core values, re-evaluating his passion for what he did, and determining then aligning with his purpose, would be his biggest motivator to succeed.
> 4. Andrew was good at being in his head for most of the day, analyzing and strategizing. Now he would be challenged to connect to people—from his heart.

Your Best Friend

If your business is not as successful as you'd like, if your people aren't motivated, or gaining and retaining customers is more arduous than ever, perhaps before you go back for your MBA for more book learning or throw in the towel of business ownership, you could discover your best friend. You'll relate to this friend's distinct assets, personal vulnerabilities, and interpersonal challenges. Because your best friend is you.

You are the friend you've ignored for too long, treating yourself like a second class citizen, hiding away, fearful of the good opinions of others.

This best friend, however, is probably shouting, "Just look at me! It's ok to be different."

Listen closely. Can you hear that voice inside? That is your authentic self speaking—the best guidance system you'll ever know.

ASK YOURSELF

When you are connected to yourself authentically, your connection with people also becomes more authentic. Authentic leadership is the most powerful and sustainable leadership of all.

The following are three questions to begin your journey toward authenticity. Take some quality time to get quiet, close your eyes, and ask yourself these questions.

Do you know who you *really* are when no one else is looking?

> 1. What are your core values?
> 2. What can you do to make your leadership more authentic?
> 3. What is your purpose?

PRACTICE THIS

As we learn more about ourselves, we grow. As we grow, our businesses naturally follow. The beauty of self-growth is that as we apply this new knowledge you won't have to work as hard and as long to get the results you want in your business and in your life. Utilize these four practices to connect to your authentic self. Then buckle up for the greatest ride of your life—getting to know your best friend will transform you forever. Watch as you lead your company forward with more confidence, power and ease.

Practice #1: Stripped Naked

Before you can discover your authentic self, you'll need to do an assessment of your strengths and weaknesses in your skill set, knowledge, and personality. Knowing your limitations can give you power. You can compensate by surrounding yourself with people who are more proficient in those areas.

Most people like their strengths and hide their weaknesses. However, it is right there, at the point of your vulnerability, that you can begin to strip away the façade that keeps you from fully be who you are—limiting your communication, self-confidence, and relating to others.

So let's get started. On a piece of paper, write down your strengths. You can use Andrew's list in the gray box as a guide:

Intelligent	Family-oriented
Strong strategy skills	Skilled at reading profit and loss
Multi-tasker	Good written communication
Forward thinker	Budgets money well
Good with numbers	Likes to problem solve
Fast learner	Hard worker
Innovative	Generous
Student of business	Soft-spoken
Strong desire to succeed	Inclusive of others
Avid reader	Good with commitments
Good organizational skills	Strong researcher

Identify at least 20 areas that are your strengths. Push yourself if you get stuck to reach that number. Ask peers, employees, business partners, or family members and friends what they consider your strengths to be.

Okay. Now comes the harder part. List your weaknesses—what you believe may limit you. Make this list extensive. Keep going, even when you think you're done. Go for at least 20. Sometimes it's the few that you eek out at the end that are the most valuable. Here is a partial list of Andrew's weaknesses:

Listening
Blame others
Delegate more
Hold my team accountable to their goals
Train and coach my team
Empower my team
Computer skills
Verbal communication
Public speaking
Introverted
Not self-confident

Next, go back to your list of weaknesses, or areas that you know you need to develop. On a scale of 1 to 10, 10 being the highest degree of weakness, write next to each how you'd rate yourself in that area. For instance, Andrew rated his listening skills as a 6. That represented that his listening was leaning to the poorer side. When answering, realize that 0 to 5 would be lesser in degree of the weakness and 6 to 10 would be greater in degree of the weakness. This is how Andrew rated himself:

Listening	6
Blame others	5
Delegate enough	5
Hold my team accountable to their goals	7
Train and coach my team	5
Empower my team	4
Verbal communicating	7
Public speaking	9
Introverted	10
Not self-confident	8

Finally, circle or highlight each weakness that you rated a 6, 7, 8, 9, or 10.

Listening	6
Blame others	5
Delegate enough	5
Hold my team accountable to their goals	7
Train and coach my team	5
Empower my team	4
Verbal communicating	7
Public speaking	9
Introverted	10
Not self-confident	8

This is the final part. Think about how you hide the highlighted weakness. What do you do so others can't see it? For example, Andrew rated his listening as a 6. This was his comment:

> Listening 6 I pretend to listen by looking at the person, but my mind is going in a million other directions.

He gave public speaking a 9. This was his comment:

> Public speaking 9 I avoid public speaking as much as I can. I know that it hurts my business, but I hate how nervous it makes me. I've really never told anyone about this before.

When you've completed Practice #1, you're ready to step out.

Practice #2: Becoming You

As a business owner and a leader, you bring personal values to your company. These values define your organization. But never should you compromise your values for the organization or for others.

Steve Jobs, the co-founder of Apple Computer, Inc., said, "The only thing that works is management by values. Find people who are competent and really bright, but more importantly, people who care exactly about the same things you care about."

Values is a word that often is confused with *value*, as in relative worth— such as, the value someone gets from buying in bulk quantity. The values I'm writing about here, however, are influential forces of how we think and behave.

To share with you just how important values can be to a leader and a company, let's take a look at Jack Welch, former CEO at General Electric Company (GE).

GE's values are so important to the chairman that he had them inscribed and distributed to all GE employees, at every level of the company. This as Welch notes:

> There isn't a human being in GE that wouldn't have the Values Guide with them. In their wallet, in their purse. It means everything and we live it. And we remove people who don't have those values, even when they post great results.[1]

Values give you defined boundaries. When you come to a crossroad and need to make a decision, you can make it based on beliefs or based on values.

Beliefs

Beliefs are experiences from the past. For instance, you put a pot with a handle in the oven. You remove it using oven mitts and then lay the mitts aside. A few minutes later you grab the pot by the handle to move it and forget that it is hot. You take your hand away quickly and probably let out a yelp as you feel the flesh in the palm of your hand burn. Rushing to the freezer, you put ice on it. The next day there is a pot that is sitting on the shelf in your cabinet. A belief would be that this pot handle is hot. Even though it hasn't been in the oven that day, you may still associate it with being hot. Pot handles are hot could be a belief. Here are some other examples of possible beliefs:

> Speeding cars can kill.
> Crossing a street on a red light can cause you physical harm.
> Eating before bedtime can make you put on weight.
> Shaking hands with a sneezing and coughing person can make you sick.
> Babies always cry.
> Employees are always asking for more money.

Beliefs come from past experiences. They aren't formulated to handle new or complex problems that you haven't yet experienced.

Values

Making a decision from your values supports what you want. It stretches beyond past experiences—beliefs—and is a better tool for more intricate problem solving. Values give you more flexibility than beliefs that limit.

Take out a piece of paper and list your values. There is no limit to the number you write. These values will be what you live and lead by. There is no compromising on them. Here is a sample list of values. Use what you'd like and create some of your own.

> trustworthy, integrity, dedicated, accountability, courageous, compassionate, persistent, dependable, responsibility, competency, equality, ambitious, honesty, empowerment, wisdom, independence, learning, influence, collaboration, teamwork, loyalty, diversity, innovativeness, fun, accomplishment

Next to each value, give an example or write why it is so important to you. Here is an example of three values from Andrew's list:

Trustworthy: I can only build a relationship with someone that I trust and someone that can trust me.
This value once distinguished and defined, then brought into action, would create great success for Andrew's company.
Integrity: I defined this value as a state of being complete or whole. I live and breathe by this value. If integrity was not present, then there is a breach that has to be addressed quickly. It keeps my team honest with each other and, therefore, honest with our customers.
Dedicated: If I have an employee who achieves results and meets his goals but isn't aligned with my values, he won't make for a long-term employee. I've discovered that when an employee isn't dedicated to my values, eventually he will leave. This costs the company because I've hired the wrong person and now have to pay for it by hiring and training someone else. Plus this employee will take our secret, competitive information to his next employer.

When leaders can identify and verbalize their values and create them as the company's values too, then they have boundaries to make decisions from them.

Post the values so all can see—even your customers. Talk about them often. Breathe them in. Be them. It is the difference between an average company and a long lasting extraordinary one.

Practice #3: Know Your Purpose

Everyone has a purpose in life. Many of us will spend an entire lifetime discovering it. Yet many still die never knowing it. Purpose brings passion—there is a reason for what you do. When times get hard, you can lean on your purpose to help you get through. It will continue to bring meaning to your work.

Extraordinary entrepreneurs know themselves. They have a balance between what they want to get done and what brings meaning to their lives. Entrepreneurs such as Ben Franklin and Thomas Edison used their life's purpose as their work—helping the world become a better place to live or contributing to the health and well-being of others.

Too often, people don't take the time to discover their purpose. This leads them to settle for what they get, instead of going for what they want. Having a purpose keeps you focused on what you want out of life. It creates a richness. You're not just coming to work; you're doing work that is more meaningful. Purpose creates meaning.

To identify your purpose, ask yourself these questions:

> What drives me?
> What makes me want to get up in the morning and get going? What makes me smile?
> Where do I want to go?
> What is that burning desire in me that I haven't spoken about because it is so big that I know it is almost impossible to achieve?

Your purpose might have nothing to do with your work. For instance, a client of mine discovered that she was passionate about ending world hunger for children. She did not have a business in the food industry like Andrew. She had never even worked in the food business. She ran a company that sold novelty items to large distributors. It had nothing to do with food, poverty, or world hunger. However, she committed a portion of her profits to a foundation that helped feed hungry children around the globe. That brought her great satisfaction. It gave meaning to her business of selling novelty items because the more she sold, the more she could contribute to her cause. It drove her. She ran a very profitable business.

To discover your purpose, you must look deeper than your daily responsibilities of working, parenting, or long-term goals. Your purpose is the ultimate reason for you to exist.

Another key to uncovering purpose may be in this question: What brings you joy?

Joy and purpose go hand in hand. It is a good path to finding your purpose. Here are some other questions to uncover your purpose:

> Have you ever watched your favorite team climb from behind to win the game? What emotions did you feel?
> Have you ever been in a stadium and watched your favorite musician or rock group appear on stage? Did you feel the roar from the audience and your own heart pounding? What was it like to sit with thousands of people all there for the same purpose—to hear the music? What emotions did it elicit?
> How did it feel to watch your child or grandchild coming into this world? Did you watch the birth? What emotions did you feel?

Recently I was travelling with my husband in Jackson Hole, Wyoming. We started out from our hotel one morning on a long drive to Yellowstone National Park. We left before sunrise. The road was dark. As we approached the park a few hours later, the sun was rising over a large lake. A mist hovered about two feet off the surface. Geese honked as they flew overhead. Wildflowers surrounding the lake were shades of yellow I hadn't seen before. New age music played on the radio. It all came together for me. It was a moment of oneness, being part of the whole. In that moment I was as small as a grain of sand and as large as the universe itself. It was very powerful—quite perfect in its simplicity. I wept.

My purpose is to help people be their most powerful selves—to help them achieve freedom, happiness, and wealth. I do this in many ways—coaching, teaching, writing, and speaking to groups. Watching people soar once they let go of obstacles and self-imposed limitations, gives me the same feeling as that early morning sunrise in Yellowstone National Park. No wonder I wept when I saw the limitlessness of the beauty in this world.

Other questions to help you identify your purpose are:

What makes me feel good about myself?
What do I love to do—what makes time fly?
What would I love to do if I didn't have to worry about money?
Where am I going?
What will I do when I get there—is it what I love to do?
What do I want my life to stand for?

Look for a pattern of similar responses. Did any of your answers bring tears to your eyes, a shiver through your body, or sudden laughter? More than likely that is the one—your purpose.

Be patient, this is a process that can take some time. Once something hits you, don't judge it. You may think that it isn't big enough—or that it is too big. Just sit with it. Be with it and let it marinate within for a few days.

Once you've identified your purpose, remind yourself during the day what it is. Write it down and post it in different places.

Watch as your life takes on new meaning. Be amazed as you feel more alive and fulfilled. Mornings will greet you with a sense of excitement. You're up to something big. Purpose and passion go hand in hand.

Practice #4: Leading from the Heart—Bring Passion

It is only with the heart that one can see rightly; what is essential is invisible to the eye.

The Little Prince by Antoine de Saint Exupéry

Passion. I love that word. It is pure energy—a lightning bolt that blasts open your whole being—the mind, body, and soul—and floods it with power. Without passion in business, most enterprises would fail, or at best achieve average performance.

Passion is the *art* of business. It is the heart and soul of a company—it's an energy force. When you love what you do, it will show. And it inspires others—motivating them to be their best. It's the opposite of the *science* of business which has a stronger focus on strategic operations and the bottom line. And yet you can't grow a strong company without both the art and the science of business.

Good entrepreneurs focus on the science of business. They may only be doers, not self-reflective. Extraordinary entrepreneurs, the most effective of our business leaders, know that it is a healthy combination of both art and science—doing and self-reflecting—that helps them to manage for the long term and to create sustainable success. They take time to ask themselves where they are going and why, and insist that their people ask those same questions for themselves.

The journey of an entrepreneur is different than most career tracks. It takes courage to become one and even more courage to continue. There are many characteristics that make up exceptional entrepreneurs. Authenticity—being who you already are, is one of them. Leading from the heart is a skill that authentic leaders bring to their organizations.

Listen to yourself and listen to others—deeply. Become a teacher. Share your life stories and your passion and purpose. Be real. People will look to you as human, like themselves—vulnerable, mistake-prone, and maybe even silly at times. Encourage people to communicate with you and with others. Insist on honesty and full self-expression. Stretch yourself. Your people will follow.

Most importantly, leading from the heart takes a lot of practice. Be patient and kind with yourself.

SUMMARY

- ☑ Remove the mask of inauthenticity.
- ☑ Honor both your strengths and your weaknesses.
- ☑ Your weaknesses will lead you to your authentic self.
- ☑ Beliefs come from past experiences.
- ☑ Values help with more complex problem solving and aren't limited by the past.
- ☑ Your purpose is why you exist.
- ☑ Look at your emotions as a guide to uncover your purpose.
- ☑ Purpose and passion go hand in hand.
- ☑ Lead from the heart to inspire and motivate others.
- ☑ Authentic leadership is the most sustainable leadership of all.

NOTE

1. Robert Slater, *Jack Welch and the GE Way: Management Insights and Leadership Secrets of the Legendary CEO* (New York: McGraw-Hill, 1999).

3

Be Do Have

If a man is called to be a street sweeper, he should sweep streets even as Michelangelo painted, as Beethoven composed music, as Shakespeare wrote poetry.

Martin Luther King, Jr.

BACKWARDS: DO HAVE BE

"I can't take vacations, I don't go out on dates, or even go to the movies with a friend," said Kiera, a talented consultant for soon-to-be college students.

"I don't have time to enjoy myself outside of work. I have time for only one thing—my plan. My plan is to become a millionaire by the time I am forty five."

Kiera, like many people, work from a *Do Have Be* concept. If I *do* what is needed to reach my goals, then I'll *have* what I want, and then I'll *be* it. Her logic is quite clear and to many that makes sense. For Kiera, it would look like this: She'll work hard and put in long hours to become a millionaire—*do*, then she'll *have* a million dollars, and she will *be* a millionaire. It's at that point that she can then take time off to create a more balanced life.

But what if it takes her beyond 45, maybe even decades to achieve her dream? Or what if she never gets there? Does that mean she'll never have a life to enjoy outside of work?

Kiera's *Do Have Be* concept was about to be blown to pieces. When that happens, and if you're alert to them, it seems like miracles will start to come out of nowhere. Let's see.

The Journey

For the past 10 years, Kiera worked for a consulting firm guiding high school students and their parents in college selection.

She had responded to an opening for a position in the consulting company as an administrative assistant. Although she had a master's degree in psychology, she found it hard to get a job that engaged both her intellectual and emotional needs. Kiera wanted to work with the adolescent population. When a position as an assistant to the owner of this boutique consulting firm opened up, she took it. To fully use her degree and to move up to a consultant level, she would have to earn her stripes. After she had celebrated her fifth year with the firm, she became a college preparation consultant.

At the age of 34, she enjoyed her work, yet had been with the firm for 10 years and was growing tired of feeling undervalued and underpaid. And as this is the motivating factor for many entrepreneurs who jump ship to start up their own company, so it was for Kiera.

The owner, unhappy to lose his prize consultant did everything possible to hold on to her. However, it was too late. Her heart was no longer with this company. In a parting conversation, her boss gave her a bonus of $10,000 and told her if it didn't work out, she would be welcomed back.

On Her Own

Kiera was a great consultant, but hadn't been tested yet as an equally talented sales person. Her role in the firm had been to deliver services while her boss did the selling. When she started her own company, she had to do both. Somehow she managed to grow the business to $150,000 in gross revenue in three years, but with marginal profits.

Kiera did little selling or marketing but instead relied on a warm network of contacts. This limited the revenue stream and was the cause for a flat profit margin. She thought that working harder would bring more success to the business. It didn't. What it did bring her was weight loss and dark circles under her eyes. There were days when she wished she could just sleep and sleep. The signs of burn-out were upon her.

Light in the Tunnel

Darryl was introduced to Kiera during his graduate school project. He did an internship with Kiera's company and she hired him upon graduation. Prior to that, he had made his way through 10 years of college part time, earning a doctorate degree in psychology, while working for a men's clothing store. Darryl knew how to sell. Even part time, he became the top salesperson for a 40 store chain. The full-timers gave Darryl much respect. He always looked energized and his eyes seemed to sparkle like he knew the secret of the world.

Working for Kiera, he became a junior consultant and was given the task of growing revenue. One year later, he had doubled sales and increased profits to 5 percent.

Kiera realized a good thing when she saw one and Darryl was one of them. She knew he was positioned to take the same path she had—to start up his own firm. She couldn't afford losing him, nor did she want to. He brought a life force to the organization, and the six other employees liked him. She made

Darryl a partner, one of the best decisions she was to ever make, for more reasons than she could presently see.

While Kiera worked harder and became more exhausted, Darryl always looked fresh and happy. Kiera was in the office at 6:00 a.m. and did not leave before 9:00 p.m. Darryl arrived at 8:30 a.m. and rarely stayed beyond 7:00 p.m. Fatigued, she grew weary of employee issues and snapped at their silly questions, while Darryl was patient, taking the time to help them. Employees rarely sought her out anymore, trying to protect her from yet another decision to make.

The Breaking Point

A high school senior and his father, a corporate head at a Fortune 500 company, came in to interview Kiera as a possible college prep consultant. She had read about the father in the news, and remembered that he helped turn-around many failing companies. Before going out to greet them, she gave herself a pep talk and glanced in the mirror to apply yet another glob of concealer under her eyes that morning. It was hopeless, she mumbled to herself. Grabbing her cup of coffee she entered into a small conference room with only a round table that sat four, placed her coffee cup down, smiled, and shook hands with the college student and the father. She had much to do to prove to them how successful she was—since her company was so small. The pressure was on and this lead to some self-doubt. But she knew her stuff and dug in as she always did. She would do whatever was needed to get this sale.

Although Kiera thought the interview went well, the father stated they'd get back to her next week after they visited other firms. A week passed and he lived up to his commitment with a follow up phone call.

"You got yourself a new client," said the father.

Kiera was happy, but the feeling of victory was short-lived. She had achieved what she had wanted—to make them her new clients. But getting to that end, only created more stress. She was adding another client to her already very full plate.

So what did she do? What she already knew how to do. She dug in again and told herself that she'd get it all done—she always did. Her philosophy of digging in and getting it done was tiring—like carrying around 50 pounds of extra weight on her back. How much longer could she work like this, she wondered?

Then, at 8:00 p.m. that night, her mother called to say that she was at the hospital. Her father was in the emergency room. They thought he'd had a heart attack. She dropped everything and ran out of the office. As the snow fell and streets were empty, she drove a seemingly slow 45 minutes to the hospital. This gave her ample time to think. Life was good, but it just wasn't working so well. She had one thing after another piling up. She knew that there would have to be a breaking point.

Kiera's father survived that night and went on to live several more healthy years. But there were many days she thought she'd soon be following in her father's path. Intense pressure filled her chest often. She wondered if stress could kill you. She didn't know how to manage her life anymore. Things were slipping through the cracks and she was on overload. The pile-up was great and she was just waiting for it all to fall apart as she managed her business, delivered services to her clients, and helped her mother care for her father.

Driven to Stress While Driving to Success

Driven entrepreneurs get things done. The problem is that in the drive to succeed and to do it all, they can put enormous pressure and stress on themselves. Some degree of pressure can be a motivator, but Kiera kept piling it on. As most of us can attest to—it can also be a deterrent and de-motivator.

Darryl knew that Kiera was digging a hole that she wouldn't be able to get out of if she kept working this way. She could only fight off exhaustion for so long before it overcame her. The light in her eyes that had initially attracted Darryl to her was gone. Her focus was cloudy, she struggled to remember details—going off on strange tangents, and her sharp perceptions on many relevant business issues were off mark. At their next monthly dinner meeting, he knew she would argue with him if he once again brought up her state of mind up, but he couldn't ignore it. However, this time when he did, Kiera didn't shush him or tell him to give her some time—that she would get it back under control. This time her eyes grew teary. She looked like a lost sheep amongst a den of lions. There was no place else to go but to surrender to Darryl's observations. He understood this. Darryl was wiser than his young years. So Kiera just let go and put her trust in Darryl.

Hours later, sitting at the same restaurant with Darryl, Kiera had a breakthrough. She saw a way out of her isolation and her misery. She was en route to blowing up her plan on how to become a millionaire, the hard way, using the *Do Have Be* concept.

The Way Out

Kiera was so busy mindlessly doing one thing after another without much joy that she never had time to just reflect. For a business leader, reflection is as equally important as taking action. Reflection allows for creativity and can bring new solutions to old problems. To make time for reflection, it must be scheduled into the work day just like any task would.

Sadly, Kiera admitted to Darryl that the car ride to the hospital to see her father was the first chance she had in a long time to really think about her life. It felt good. She wanted to do it more often. But she knew that as soon as she stepped foot back in her office the next day, desire would fade and it would all be forgotten. She had things to do and work to complete.

Kiera watched Darryl work and was amazed at his efficiency. It seemed so easy for him to get things done and he always had such a relaxed good nature. People gravitated toward him. He made selling appear so easy. She couldn't understand how he could appear so relaxed since there was so much pressure for him to produce results. His goals for the year were set as a stretch, yet he was making every milestone along the way. With the tension of the economic recession looming in the background and high performance goals set, how was he able to appear so relaxed and happy?

BE DO HAVE

Darryl spoke to her about a concept that he used to help him stay balanced. He practiced it a lot during peak times, when everything was flowing and going his way. He found that the more he practiced it during these times, the more natural it was to use during difficult times. It helped him to remain centered while achieving his goals. Darryl explained the paradigm of *Do Have Be*. He told her that she was working the hard way to get things done.

"You think to become a millionaire you have to do all the things you need to do and that will bring you millions. That's called *Do Have Be*. It is the paradigm most people work in—except the smart ones," he said with a chuckle.

"There is a smarter way and you already see how it works because you admire my easy flow as I continue to achieve success."

"Are you open to it?" he asked Kiera.

Kiera said yes.

Be Do Have is the paradigm Darryl uses. He told Kiera that right on the other side of her problem is the answer.

"The question you must ask yourself, then, is 'who do I have to be to see the solution?' " stated Darryl.

Darryl

When Darryl had first started out selling men's clothing, he was a young kid in high school, stocking shelves at night. After school, he would come to work early to watch the sales people on the floor. He was fascinated at how they could talk customers into buying suits, and how they earned a living selling. When he entered college, he applied for a position in sales at the same company. In one month, the sales manager was on the verge of firing him— and told him so. He wasn't even near his quota for the month. Darryl couldn't understand why he wasn't able to sell. He was trying hard, working long hours, and he was an engaging talker. Yet, he was struggling to make enough money to pay for college.

In a desperate last hope on a slow rainy day, he cornered Joe, the top sales person in the company and fired question after question at him. When he and Joe were done talking, Darryl realized that he been going about selling backwards. He was using the *Do Have Be* paradigm that we all learn as children. It is the same concept that Kiera was using to become a millionaire.

Darryl was waiting until he could sell a lot of suits to become a success. Joe told him to read Napoleon Hill's book, *Think and Grow Rich*,[1] or Charles Haanel's book, *The Master Key System*.[2] Both spoke about first *being* successful before you even put a dollar in your pocket. First Darryl would have to think, act, and talk like he was a successful salesman who sold men's clothing, before he actually became one.

"Sort of like faking it 'til you make it," he told Kiera.

That night Darryl left work, drove immediately to the bookstore and bought the books. He read each one cover to cover and didn't sleep. One of the quotes from Haanel's book stood out.

> The attitude of mind necessarily depends upon what we think. Therefore, the secret of all power, all achievement and all possession depends upon our method of thinking.
>
> We must "be" before we can "do," and we can "do" only to the extent which we "are," and what we "are" depends upon what we "think."

It worked. Six months later, Darryl exceeded his quota and became the number one salesperson in the 40 store chain.

Once Darryl relaxed and stopped trying so hard, he was able to focus longer on the customer—listening more deeply, thinking more creatively, and identifying their needs.

Kiera's Breakthrough

At their dinner meeting, Darryl asked Kiera what she could do to start feeling better. Kiera said that she really needed to take a break. Darryl then asked what was stopping her from doing that. She said when she had achieved her goal of becoming a millionaire, she could rest more. Darryl told her that she had it in reverse.

With the effort she was putting in and the pressure increasing, it would take her longer time than was necessary to get to the level of success she wanted so desperately. Plus, she would probably burn out well before she got there.

Most people will create a result that they want to achieve and then identify and perform actions to get there. They will do something to become something. But Darryl was about to share with the Kiera the concept that changed his life. Instead of just doing things to become a millionaire, first become one.

Where's the Puck?

Here's an example of *Be Do Have*. Suppose you want to lose weight. First you'll determine how much you want to lose, then you begin to diet and exercise and monitor your weight loss. After two or three months, or maybe even before that, you lose interest if it's taking too long. That is the *Do Have Be* paradigm. You'll *do* what is necessary to *have weight loss* and then you'll *be* thin and fit. But that's the more difficult way because initially you're fighting your own self-image of being overweight. Instead, first adopt a sense of well-being and fitness as if you're already there. *I am thin*, or *I am fit*, or *I look great with no clothes on*. Now you're ready to do what's necessary to get there. This is the path of least resistance.

Be Do Have in weight loss is the same model that Darryl took on when he couldn't sell. But once he changed his mindset from being the kid who just stocked shelves trying to sell clothing, to the mindset of a star salesperson, his sales soared.

Becoming a Millionaire

If Kiera wants to be a millionaire, she must first become one in her mind. How? She can read about them, talk to them, or observe them. Find out how they act, talk, and think. She must breathe it all in. She must feel it in every cell of her body.

Wayne Gretzky, one of the greatest ice hockey players in history said, "I skate to where the puck is going to be, not where it has been."

Be like Gretsky. He already took the winning shot in his mind, before he even skated to the puck. Maybe that is why Hill titled his book, *Think and Grow Rich*, not *Grow Rich, then Think*.

ASK YOURSELF

If you can feel in every fiber of your body what it would be like to be where you want to be, you're taking the first step to making it happen. Not only will you reach your goal with less effort and in shorter time, but it will be a more enjoyable ride. After all, most successful people claim it's not about the destination—it's about the journey. Start enjoying the journey more!

Take some quality time to get quiet, close your eyes, and ask yourself these questions.

1. What are five results or goals that I currently want to achieve?
2. What is stopping me from getting there?
3. How do I feel when I keep trying to reach these goals and I don't make them?
4. How would I feel if I reached those goals? Really describe your feelings.

PRACTICE THIS

Be Do Have is a tool that can help you realize your dreams. Simple sounding, it may be awkward at first to initiate because it is like riding a bike. Until you practice, at first you may fall often. But don't give up—it will be well worth the effort. The following four practices will help you to incorporate this concept into getting the results you want, all that you desire. You will need to take each step in order, so don't skip ahead.

Practice #1: Clarify Your Goals

Get more of what you want and less of what you don't want. Here is the first step in making that happen. Identify goals. Write them down. Some of your goals may be easy to visualize, like *make more money*. But notice that I said clarify your goals. You'll need to break them down. If making more money is a goal, state how much you want to make and by when. For example, do you want to become a millionaire before you turn a particular age? What age is that? Get crystal clear on what you want to have and by when.

Practice #2: Fake It 'til You Make It

Once you've clarified your goals, it's time for the fun part. You're going to fake it 'til you make it. Here's how to fake it. Imagine you've reached your goal: *I'm a millionaire at 35.* The first part of faking it is to visualize having it, even though you don't. Find a comfortable chair in a quiet place. Close your eyes. It's best to close your eyes because you'll cut out distractions of the real world.

Choose one of your goals. We'll use, *I'm a millionaire at 35.* Now visualize that you've done it. You've reached your goal. You've reached being a millionaire and you're only 35 years old.

These questions will help you to fake it:

> How does it feel?
> What do you have?
> What does it look like?
> What will you do with it?
> Will it be used for fun or business?
> How will you act?
> How would you carry yourself?
> How would you treat others?
> How much more confident would you be?
> How much more would you go out of your way to help others? How good would that feel?

Really imagine it all as you respond to those questions. The longer you can allow it to come in, the more real your mind will make it. That's what you want.

Let's take a look at Kiera's visualization process. She wants to become a millionaire by age 45. Kiera's questions to herself will include these:

> What will it be like to feel that money in my hands?
> What does it feel like to see it all stacked up on the table in front of me?
> *(continued)*

What does it feel like to be able to buy whatever I want without worry?
What will I buy?
How much will I put into a savings account?
Who will help me to invest it and where do I want to invest it? Will I give any of it away to family?
Will I buy a new home? What will that look like? Describe every room. Describe the outside of the home. Who will live in the home with me? Will I have a mortgage? If not, what will it feel like not to have to pay a mortgage each month?
Will I buy a new car? Can I smell the leather interior? What color is my shiny new car? How is the sound system? Can I hear my favorite song playing on it—coming out of the all the speakers?
Will I donate some money to my favorite charity? Will I do that anonymously? Or will it be more fun to watch them as they open up the envelope and pull out my check?

Kiera may imagine walking into the finest shops on Madison Avenue in New York City. She'll pull out her wallet with thousands of dollars in it and pay cash for that new piece of jewelry knowing that she has more saved up earning interest in the bank. What does it like to never have to worry about not having enough money ever again?

Visualize your goal by asking questions and imagining the answers. Imagine all the fun you'll have by reaching that goal. Remember you're going to fake it—allow yourself to do that. Keep asking questions until it begins to feel real. Your mind won't know the difference.

Practice #3: Shift the Paradigm

Most people who want to achieve a goal create a strategic action plan with a to-do list; these are actions to take in order to realize the goal. The to-do list is essential to create, but has one problem. If you haven't shifted who you are *being* while taking actions to complete your to-do list, you're running backwards up the hill. You're doing it the hard way. To create less tension and more ease and fun in reaching your goal, let's create another list. This list is called a to-be list, who you want to be each day.

For example, we all can get critical of ourselves from time to time. Just look in the mirror. Do you look at your defects? Of course you do. It's hard to resist. After all, maybe they have improved overnight.

Do you judge your work poorly? Perhaps you don't think your writing is so hot, but you promised to submit an article. You read what you've written and judge yourself. *I can't write, this is no good, if only I could write like* _____. Fill in the blank. Maybe you create a distraction to get up from your computer. You go get something to eat or open the mail, anything to divert you from writing. These are sabotaging thoughts and actions that take you away from the goal of writing your article. So one of the things on your to-be list is to be kinder to yourself and less judgmental. To begin being kinder, start by doing it over the next hour, then the next two hours. Before you know it, you'll be doing it more often.

This practice requires an internal shift to get you to your goals faster and with less resistance. You'll have to take a closer look at how you are *being* then take action to shift it.

Once you've visualized the end result—reaching your goal, knowing how it will feel, and what you will do once you're there—you're ready to *be* in that result, to live it, before it is even actualized. How much fun is that!

As you take on this practice, remember to keep in mind the visualization process that you applied in Practice #2.

As an example, this is Kiera's to-be list.

Positive attitude
Observer of people
Compassionate
Appreciative
Patient
Good listener, putting myself in the speaker's shoes
Clear communicator
Love myself, no matter what
Give up judging and criticizing
Think abundance
Be kind
Stop doubting myself
Do what I promise
Live as a student of business and life
Give up having to be right
Give up having to know it all
Feel successful
Let go of struggle

At first this list may appear more like a wish list. That's fine. Maybe you're already trying to be like some of the items you've listed, you'd really like to, but can't seem to get there. That's fine too. Just create your wish list of how you'd love to be.

Each day read and add to your to-be list. Keep adding to it as you think of more ways you'd like to be.

Take one item on your to-be list each day and *be it* for that day. For example, today you may choose to be less judgmental of yourself. Write that down on a three by five card and carry it around all day. If you're at your desk, put it in front of you so that you can't help but look at it and remind yourself to be less judgmental. When a critical thought comes to mind, tell yourself it isn't true. Then counter it with a positive comment, such as, *I enjoy how I cook or take care of my garden. I like that I take time to spend with my children.*

An internal shift gets created immediately. Don't worry if you don't see results immediately. They're on the way!

Each day choose another item on your to-be list. If you'd like you can use the same item for more than one day. When the shift occurs, it will take less thought, becoming more automatic. Eventually it will become part of you—no thought needed.

Practice #4: Enjoy the Ride

Getting to where you want to be—attaining your goal can be done with difficulty or ease. Either way, it's your choice. Really it is. You see you can choose the difficult ride—one of stress, pressure, and working hard. Or you can choose the path that is filled with peace. I don't know anyone who would choose the former.

Your destination will give you what you want. But the journey will teach you who you really are. It will show you your strengths and your vulnerabilities, one as important as the other.

One summer while traveling through New England, my son who was about to enter medical school, and my daughters, eleven and nine, decided to climb Mt. Washington.

Mount Washington

National Geographic published an article on Mount Washington in February, 2009 on their Web site, they wrote:

> New Hampshire's 6,288-foot Mount Washington, home to some of the most extreme weather conditions on the planet and the site of the fastest wind gusts ever recorded on the surface of the earth, is the subject of a feature article in the February edition of National Geographic magazine. . . .
>
> National Geographic illustrates that New Englanders and visitors need to look no further than their own backyard to find Arctic conditions that rival any other extreme location on the planet.[3]

This gives you a preview of what was to come.

My children had decided to climb Mt. Washington without considering us, their parents. Horrified by the thought of our three children climbing this treacherous mountain by themselves, yet not wanting to do the full climb to the top, my husband and I decided we just had to do it. As we began our climb, the summit became our destination. What started as a strenuous hike, turned into six hours of physical and mental challenges.

We had never climbed to the summit of a mountain before, nevertheless a mountain with the formidable reputation of Mount Washington. A mountain with a dark side—the number of human lives lost over the years rivals the number of deaths on Mt. Everest. Most fatalities can be attributed to the mountain's harsh weather. To support this fact, plaques line the walls of the summit's observatory with names of people who had died on the mountain, including year and cause of death, such as avalanche, fall, or hypothermia. I was glad that the plaque was not posted at the bottom of the mountain. I would never have done the climb!

Journey to the Summit

Our journey to the summit was rigorous. We had to work together as a team, supporting each other as doubts crept in. Doubts are one of the worst things that can happen while climbing. They influence and impede your confidence and judgment. We also had to support each other physically. No one told us about the weather before we traversed this mountain. And we hadn't had time to research it.

My nine-year-old daughter was convinced she could climb in shorts. As we made our way up and the summer temperature dropped from 80° to freezing, I had to share my hat and woolen mittens with her. I wore one mitten and she wore the other one. When her ears were warm, she gave me my hat back to warm mine. We had to make team decisions about proceeding or turning back during the lightning and rain storms we faced. If we were to proceed, we knew there wouldn't be shelter because we were above the tree line. It was barren near the top.

We did it. Reaching the summit was a memorable experience. One that none of us will forget. But it was the richness of the journey—our trials and tribulations, our tears and laughter, that brought us this unforgettable memory.

SUMMARY

- ☑ Make your goals crystal clear.
- ☑ Be what you want to have.
- ☑ Envision what you want.
- ☑ Notice how it looks and feels to have achieved it—if only in your mind.
- ☑ Fake it 'til you make it.
- ☑ Create a to-be list.
- ☑ The journey will bring you greater lessons than getting to your destination, even though in the moment it may not look like it will.
- ☑ Enjoy the ride.

NOTES

1. Napoleon Hill, *Think and Grow Rich!* (San Diego: Aventine Press, 2004).

2. Charles Haanel, *The Master Key System* (Radford, VA: Wilder Publications, 2007).

3. Neil Shea, "Backyard Artic," *National Geographic*, February 2009, http://ngm.nationalgeographic.com/2009/02/mt-washington/shea-text.

4

Put Your Ego to Sleep

Be humble for you are made of earth. Be noble for you are made of stars.

Serbian Proverb

ASSET OR HINDRANCE

Admit it. Entrepreneurs have healthy egos. We have to if we're to survive the rocky road we'll traverse. If you're shaking your head in denial—yet you've taken the path of starting your own business faced with ups and downs, and at times, seemingly insurmountable mountains to climb, you're one of us. As I interviewed entrepreneurs for this book, I found an interesting phenomenon occurring. There were those who proudly admitted they had a strong ego and would hold on tight to it. Then there were others who timidly denied that their ego had played a part in their success (could they be the exception to humanity, and not even have one?), but when pressed further, reticently confessed.

Dipak, the owner of a successful Web development company who had started his business during the technology boom and survived, was in the former group. Dipak claimed that his industry chewed up and spit out those who didn't have survival skills. To make it through the boom years and to keep going, took a special combination of shrewdness and talent. Dipak knew he had both. That said, he not only survived the churn, he landed flat on his feet as the economy stabilized.

Dipak declared that it was his ability to be flexible and roll with the punches that helped him through the turbulence of that era. But there was another matter—his ego.

A healthy ego can help us win business, stand our ground when confronted by a competitor, or take on the persona of a successful business owner. The ego has another side to it also. Because it is *me driven*—the ego wants us to be seen as the best, the smartest, the strongest, the most competitive, the most recognized, or the one with the most material gains. This is the side that also keeps us separate from others, and more competitive. In many instances, such as in building a team, keeping ourselves separate and better than others, just won't cut it.

Dipak had all the accoutrements of success—a Porsche convertible and an SUV, a million dollar home, a beach house and a mountain cabin, a fine art collection, and two children and a wife. He was as proud of his perfect children who went to up-scale private schools and his beautiful wife who shopped for her seasonal wardrobes in the high-end stores of New York City, as he was of his possessions. Some people commented that his family was treated as another belonging. However, for Dipak this was just another way to show the world how successful he had become.

Dipak never considered his ego a hindrance. Contrarily, he saw it as an asset. It helped him build a successful business and traverse through difficult times, blindly leading him through storms—instilling in him a continued confidence in his abilities. He fed off of his ego and his ego grew from his feedings. Yet just as his ego had helped him to become successful, it would soon become an unexpected encumbrance.

Riding the Wave

Born in Mumbai, India, when Dipak was 11 his parents moved to the United States where he attended school and later became an American citizen. He took great pride in his ability to excel in science. After graduating from Massachusetts Institute of Technology, he realized his first career goal and took an entry level job in the field of technology. In 1996, after several years of working in the IT department for a financial organization, Dipak set out to do what he always knew he would do—to build his own successful company. His timing was perfect. He started a Web development business out of his home at the height of the dot-com boom. When he hit the $5 million mark, his wife, Suri, left her job and came to work in his business, managing human resources and the office. Within a short time, Dipak purchased a building and was running a healthy $10 million company with 30 employees.

The Turning Tides

If you knew Dipak during those years, you couldn't deny his huge ego, said many of his friends and colleagues.

"Dipak had only one love in his life—Dipak," they declared.

As he was interviewed in magazines and newspapers for his entrepreneurial genius, his ego continued to be happily nourished. Dipak became a whiz kid icon who people either loved or hated. He had a no-nonsense approach to dealing with anyone—you were either with him or against him. And you didn't want to be against him. He was a fierce competitor. He had a force within him that wouldn't be denied. Dipak got what he wanted. Nothing could get in the way. And so it was that Dipak's strong ego created a burning desire to win while blinding him to his arrogance.

A colleague told Dipak that if he made it through the initial wild and glorious years of the technology boom, yet continued to partner with his inflated ego in personal triumphs and glory, he would eventually be bound by dependent employees who relied on him for every move they made. It is rare for people who have big egos to allow others to shine or be smarter or better. In Dipak's wake, his employees were just robots, taking orders and fulfilling on them.

And then it finally happened. For everything that peaks must also eventually flush out the excess. The dot-com bubble burst. Dipak survived while many other start-ups shut down. Once again, Dipak, the self-promoting superstar took center stage, pleased that he had sustained the upheaval of the times, while many of his competitors had lost everything. He loved the spotlight of being at the top, the victorious winner. Just Dipak (and his ego) standing there alone, quite happy—leaving his employees in the perpetual position of looking up at him.

As the dust settled over the next several years and the weakest companies were plucked from the batch, Dipak noticed sales were slowly dropping in his company. Thinking this was a quirk, he ignored it. Each month the numbers showed up worse than the month before. Slowly he began to become concerned. Was a pattern developing here, he thought?

In Dipak-style, he put on his impenetrable shield of bravado, self-confidence (and ego), and tried to rally his team into performance. Trained to rely on Dipak for all the answers and always micro-managed in the past, his team was lost. As he pushed them harder for results, they became resentful instead of motivated. They weren't used to being asked to think for themselves.

As success diminished, so did Dipak's relationships. No one felt obligated to put up with his egotistic personality. They regarded him as a saint who had fallen and was now a tyrant. As hard as Dipak tried to understand why he couldn't pull his team together he never looked at his own behavior. He didn't listen well, never took feedback to heart, and had an attitude of a know-it-all. Blaming people on his team for poor performance caused employee dissatisfaction and many of them quit. When Dipak's company went into the red, for the first time in his life he didn't have any answers and sunk into an almost comatose state.

From Confidence to Uncertainty

You don't have to have an ego as extreme as Dipak's to have it cause destruction. For Dipak, not even his ego could help bail him out this time. Money was flying out the window faster than Dipak could calculate. He had to cut expenses drastically. On top of that, Dipak and Suri lost all of their investments. So sure of technology's growth, they had bought shares of stock in only hi-tech companies. The stocks soared during the boom days, but when the market crashed, they lost it all. Gone were their savings, retirement, and college funds. Forced to sell their two vacation homes, they were left with the home they lived in and the business.

Without the security of his investments and savings, Dipak moved from a mindset of confidence to one of uncertainty. Searching for answers, his ego (instead of being a force and guiding light) became an impediment.

THE EGO

False Sense of Self

Ego is a Latin word which means *I myself*. According to Sigmund Freud in his book, *The Ego and the Id*,[1] the mind has three structures: the id, the ego, and the superego. While the id represents our primal drives and the superego represents right from wrong, the ego is the bridge between the two and gives us a sense of self.

Today, however, popular parlance uses the word ego to represent one's self-esteem or self-worth. We might say that someone like Dipak has a big ego or an unrealistic sense of himself.

If success is driven by passion, beliefs, and a healthy ego, then it is important to keep one's ego in check. If not, while achieving success, an inflated ego can give us a false sense of ourselves. For instance, it may lead us to think that we succeeded on our own, without the help of other people. Of course, this wouldn't be true if you are leading a company and have other people on your team.

The ego won't want you to discern this. It is out to win, leaving others in the dust. So when Dipak needed his team to become more independent thinkers, they didn't know how because he had always been the golden child, thinking for them. As Dipak became more successful in the public eye, he grabbed on to all the positive press that glorified him. He developed a false sense of himself. *I did this all on my own. I am the best. No one can do it like me. No one can come close to who I am.*

The Balancing Element: Humility

Dipak had relied on his inflated ego to tell him who he was, so when failure came, he didn't know who he was anymore. His ego now was telling him that he was worthless and not valued. To maintain good mental health and strong relationships, he was missing an important element that would balance out the ego; humility.

Humility is one of the two characteristics in Level 5 leaders that Jim Collins writes about in his book *Good to Great*.[2] Collins states that humility is one of the distinguishing factors (the other being *will*) among CEOs who took companies from good or very good performance (Level 4 leader) to enduring excellence (Level 5 leader).

In an article for the *Harvard Business Review*, Collins writes:

> How do Level 5 leaders manifest humility? They routinely credit others, external factors, and good luck for their companies' success. But when

results are poor, they blame themselves. They also act quietly, calmly, and determinedly—relying on inspired standards, not inspiring charisma, to motivate.[3]

Dr. Mike Armour in his LeaderPerfect Newsletter states this:

Humility lets us dismiss concerns about being the center of attention, so that we can step aside and let others shine. People don't tend to trust people who insist on taking all the credit or hogging the spotlight.

Humility leaves us open to what others can teach us, no matter what their station in life. As a result we learn and develop wisdom more quickly, because we allow others to be our mentor.

Humility lets us treat even difficult people with such respect that in turn they feel more worthwhile. People do not typically invest their trust in someone who makes them feel invisible or insignificant.

Humility preserves a spirit of gratitude. A spirit of gratitude does more than perhaps any other character trait to keep our outlook on life positive and healthy. Sensing this, people are unlikely to put great trust in a leader who is ungrateful, for (unconsciously, at least) they realize that ingratitude is a sign of other character flaws.

Humility allows us to confront our own failings and take valuable lessons from them. Nothing is more harmful to trust than a leader who lives in denial or who never learns from things done poorly.

Humility allows us to be more patient with those who are still learning and thus prone to mistakes. We see in them a reflection of our own need to learn and improve. Appropriate patience is critical in building trust, for impatience breeds anxiety and even fear among those we lead, the very antithesis of trust.

Humility makes us approachable and receptive to being held accountable. Leaders who hold others accountable must be open and willing to be held accountable themselves. Otherwise, a double standard is at work that is inimical to trust.

Humility keeps our curiosity alive. Aware of how much we don't know, recognizing that we have our own pattern of blind spots, we are eager to explore and learn. After all, people don't normally trust "know-it-alls."

As you review this list of ways in which humility contributes to trust-building, you will notice that many of them relate to learning. Learning from others. Learning from mistakes. Learning from being held accountable. Learning by keeping curiosity high.

It's this distinct relationship between humility and learning that makes it so critical for leaders who want to propel an organization to sustained peak performance. The faster we learn as leaders, the quicker we can take our organization to the top.[4]

Loss of Self

An inflated ego justifies what we think is right—even when it's not. Big egos want recognition for being the best. Humility wins over followers, builds trust and strong relationships. The balance of the two was what Dipak was missing.

No one would have called Dipak humble. He would have to change if he wanted his company to survive. Worse, if he wasn't going to bring about more humility to his daily actions and way of being, the universe, as our ultimate purveyor of lessons, would step in and do it for him. Because Dipak was unaware of who he was being and how to change, when his company started to fail, the universe was ready to provide him a wake-up call.

Most people measure their worth on the basis of what they do, their achievements, and their reputation. When Dipak's world fell apart, he lost all of that. Since he valued himself for what he had achieved, when he lost it, he also lost his sense of self. That is the danger of the ego. If you put much weight on material gains, when you lose them, you're not sure who you are without them.

Defending the Turf

In his psychoanalytic theory, Freud noted that a defense mechanism is a tool the ego develops to protect against anxiety. Defense mechanisms will protect the mind from emotions and thoughts that are too intense to deal with at the moment. We may consciously use a defense mechanism to reduce anxiety, such as *denial* when accused of a wrong doing. However, most times we are not conscious when we use a defense mechanism. When asked if you took a cookie off of the cookie plate, you may respond guiltily, *I didn't do it*. A defense mechanism may also be used subconsciously, such as in Dipak's case. When this happens the truth is avoided or gets distorted. More problems then arise.

In the gray box is a list of defense mechanisms. The first 10 were identified by Anna Freud.[5] The last six are additional defense mechanisms.

Defense Mechanisms

1. Denial: refusal to know or admit something; or something said, believed, or assumed to be false.
2. Repression: keeping information out of our conscious awareness.
3. Displacement: taking out our frustration and emotions on others who are less intimidating.
4. Sublimation: changing from acting out on harmful impulses to something less harmful and more tolerable.
5. Projection: displacing our feelings on to another person.
6. Intellectualization: thinking in a more scientific, less emotional way.
7. Rationalization: avoiding the truth about a situation by explaining it in a logical manner.
8. Regression: acting out with more child-like behaviors.
9. Reaction formation: hiding true feelings by acting the opposite way.

(continued)

10. Suppression: trying to forget something that causes you anxiety.
11. Acting out: taking action rather than thinking things through.
12. Avoidance: not confronting the offensive situation.
13. Passive-Aggressive: expressing anger indirectly.
14. Humor: expressing sarcasm or the funny parts of circumstances.
15. Compensation: over-achieving in an area to balance failure in another area.
16. Altruism: helping others to gratify self.

Dipak's Defenses

Dipak blamed the downward spiral in the technology world and his team for the company's existing failure, never once looking at himself. His team's collective thinking had been squashed by his superstardom and now when he needed them, they were paralyzed. He couldn't motivate them. The more he relied on his ego, pretending to put up a false front, pretending he felt confident, the more people could see through his veil.

A Healthy Ego

What does an entrepreneur do when his almighty ego gets in the way? He needs to put it to sleep. What Dipak had to discover—what every experienced, awakened entrepreneur comes to understand—is that his ego can only take him so far. Then it becomes a detriment, if not kept in balance. Dipak was to discover that his ego may have encouraged some outward growth, but it stifled inner development—his own personal development and the self awareness of others' needs. Without inner development, it was impossible for his company to keep growing.

Dipak is an example of a dynamic entrepreneur who was on his way to great success. But because his success came from a self-centered core of gathering people, money, and achievements for his own gain, it would not, could not last. Eventually it caught up with him.

A healthy ego balances confidence and humility. True confidence is a quiet knowing. It is so quiet that others may think they've had the success, or gotten there on their own, and we allow for that. A healthy ego is not about proving how great we are.

If Dipak was to keep his company from closing, he would need to anesthetize his ego and put it to sleep, in order to build inner growth that would help him to develop long term relationships with others.

The real voyage of discovery and growth consists not in seeing new landscapes but in having new eyes.

Marcel Proust

ASK YOURSELF

Take some quality time to get quiet, close your eyes, and ask yourself these questions.

Did you ever . . .

1. Find yourself trying to win an argument—you just have to win?
2. Drive your car and turn up the music, wanting people to notice you, or your car?
3. Take all the credit for a shared task or project?
4. Interrupt someone while they were talking because something they said reminded you of something you had done, and anyway the other person was talking too much and you were getting bored?
5. Have someone on your team try to stand up to you, giving you another point of view, but you shot them down?

PRACTICE THIS

A big ego doesn't serve anyone. In the long run, it can actually create a breakdown in trust and damage relationships. You can't be a superstar and also build a team. The following practices will help you put your ego to sleep in order to build strength in your company and a team of people who trust you. Read one of these each day. Then practice it for a day or even a week. When you've exhausted that one and you're ready, move on to the next practice.

Practice #1: When You're Fighting the Good Fight, Stop

In order to keep feeding your ego, you must get more, do more, be more, or win more. When you don't feed it, you are *less than*, according to the ego. You're less than others, or less than who you think you should be. The ego fears being less than.

It also fears losing. When you pursue winning, you'll always lose. Because eventually someone will be younger, better looking, wealthier, or smarter at business. When you realize that, you'll feel the worthlessness it causes.

Even if you enjoy competing for the fun of it, you don't have to stay *the winner* in your mind. If you're the winner, then other people are the losers. And if others are losers, you'll always feel superior to them. Superior people aren't much fun to be around for very long. And they certainly don't build loyal, long-lasting relationships and teams.

As you shift from pursuing to win to contributing to others, you may just get more victories with less effort while winning and retaining new relationships.

Become aware of your impulse to win, gain recognition, or get more stuff. If you can notice this while you're right in the middle of doing it, great. Recognize the impulse, then stop—don't act on it. Instead, let the other person *win*. Give them the recognition, even if you feel you're the one who deserves it. Give up having to win.

At first this may be hard. You'll feel as though you're giving up something important. But you're not. It is only your ego at work, making you the victor and the other the loser. When you give to someone else without wanting anything in return, you're always the winner. It's karma. Eventually it will come back to you in spades; it always does. Just remember that karma shouldn't be the reason why you're doing it because then you're defeating the purpose of this practice.

Practice #2: If They Don't Love You, It Doesn't Matter

You can't control what other people think of you or what they say. Try asking various people their thoughts and opinions of your new ad or the team you put in place to get your new project off the ground. More than likely they will each have a different opinion.

So, what really matters? *How you feel about yourself.*

Remember that the *good* opinion of others, is just that—their opinion. It is not yours. I know it's not easy to disregard criticism, especially when it's directed at you. But it's important to learn to do so. It will bring you great freedom and internal peace.

Knowing your flaws, as well as your strengths creates confidence. For instance, let's say that you know you aren't great at negotiating, especially with vendors. In fact, you know that you have this soft side that keeps you from getting tougher around pricing.

Your partner says, "How could you have negotiated such an awful price?

It looks like we'll have to dig deeper into our budget and make some cuts in other areas."

You hear it as, "You screwed up. Can't you get things right? Because you didn't negotiate a good price, we have to forfeit on other critical things needed for the business."

But if you know that negotiating isn't your strong suit, then instead of getting offended or flustered by his comment, you just shrug, lessening any tension and knowing that your weakness, or naiveté to negotiate with strength, presents itself once again.

You can reply confidently to your partner, "You're so right. I should have gotten you involved at that point. Remind me next time."

That's freedom.

When you can detach from the criticisms of others, you can see more clearly, without defending the areas that you'd like to improve.

You can even laugh at yourself. We all have weaknesses; it's part of being human.

When you can shield the criticisms directed at you, you'll be able to see more clearly the issues of the criticizer. Perhaps as a child, someone made "the criticizer" feel stupid or inadequate. It could have been a coach, teacher, parent, sibling, or friend. Now he projects that onto others, many times unknowingly. When you can dodge the remark and get clear that it isn't true, you remain centered. This not only helps you, but also stops a series of reactions from both you and your criticizer.

When your partner questioned your negotiating, instead of reacting, you might try this.

"You're right. I'm not great at negotiating, especially with John. He's such a nice person and I don't want to hurt his feelings. I know that I shouldn't bring that into my negotiations with John. I'm going to do some reading on negotiations. Do you have a book you'd recommend?"

Timing is everything, so read body language and tone to be sure that it is the right time to be asking your partner reflective questions. If he seems calm, you may also add this.

"You had a strong reaction to the way I negotiated. What happened? What did that bring up?"

You may have opened up a window for your partner to admit he is concerned, maybe even scared about the financial situation of the company. Because you are thinking clearly and not reacting, you have the ability to not only help yourself, but also your partner. Instead of a battle of the egos, it is a lesson that can provide understanding, compassion, and alignment.

The opinions of others certainly can stump hard on our egos. When the ego is aroused and feels it needs to defend, anger and hurt are usually feelings brought to the surface, if we're not aware. When you harness your ego's knee-jerk reaction, you'll end up feeling more powerful because you are free.

Practice #3: See Things with New Eyes

You may be asking yourself, "If I don't win or have more, then who am I?"

Instead of seeing yourself through the eyes of what you have or don't have, change your lens.

Look through the lens of what you do have. Appreciate what you have already. Your ego will constantly tell you that you need more. You'll never have enough. If you're always working toward getting more or being better than others, you'll never be happy because it is an uphill battle that never ends. As you appreciate what you have and stop looking at what you don't have yet, more will come to you. This isn't *airy-fairy*. This is real. I've seen it happen over and over again for not only myself, but for the people I coach.

Learn to give to others what *you* want to have. For example, if *you* want to be respected, then give more respect to others and respect will begin to show up at your doorstep, quite magically.

Practice #4: Say Goodbye to Your Old Friend

As you take less credit for your accomplishments, you'll have more time to achieve and will have more success. When you allow your ego to make you believe you're the greatest and the other person isn't, you'll always be looking over your shoulder and never be free.

Let go of being right. Let go of trying to win. Let go of the constant battle to purchase more things. Let go of wanting to hear good things about yourself from others. Let go of letting others know that you did something good for another. Let go of being better than others. Let go of knowing it all. Let go of having to be the superstar—instead let others shine.

I know this will be hard at first. Perhaps very hard. That's why I've called these *practices*. The more you practice, the better you'll get.

Practice #5: Differentiate Heart-felt from Mind-felt

Mind-felt feelings are judgmental and they seek facts and information, such as in problem solving. Think of, WIIFM, or What's In It For Me? What do I get from this? Is this good for me? Mind-felt is intellectually based.

When building relationships, mind-felt feelings aren't the best tools to call upon. They tend to separate us from others (such as defending or arguing our point of view), instead of connecting us together. Elements of the heart or heart-felt feelings, such as compassion, trust, humility, appreciation, and love, support strong relationships with others and are nonjudgmental. Language or intellect cannot truly describe these elements; they are more equivalent to intuition and a higher wisdom. Authenticity, genuineness, and integrity are present in heart-felt feelings.

When you find your ego ready to leap into action to defend, justify your position, or rationalize your behavior, pull out your tool bag of mind-felt feelings. Connecting with someone (heart-felt) versus pushing them away (mind-felt) will create greater satisfaction and more inner peace.

SUMMARY

- ☑ Ego gives you an inflated, false sense of self.
- ☑ Humility is the balancing element to ego.
- ☑ If you come from an over inflated ego, when you lose, you feel less than or worthless.
- ☑ A healthy ego balances confidence and humility.
- ☑ The ego resides in the part of the mind that houses consciousness.
- ☑ Defense mechanisms protect the mind from emotions and thoughts that are too intense to deal with at the moment.
- ☑ We use defense mechanisms to reduce anxiety.
- ☑ Put your ego to sleep.
- ☑ Acknowledge and include others in your success.
- ☑ Learn to differentiate mind-felt from heart-felt for inner peace.

NOTES

1. Sigmund Freud and James Strachey, *The Ego and the Id (The Standard Edition of the Complete Psychological Works of Sigmund Freud)* (New York: W. W. Norton & Company, 1990).

2. Jim Collins, *Good to Great: Why Some Companies Make the Leap . . . and Others Don't* (New York: HarperCollins Publishers, 2001).

3. Jim Collins, "Level 5 Leadership, The Triumph of Humility and Fierce Resolve," *Best of Harvard Business Review*, BR 2001:1.

4. Mike Armour, "Humility and Leadership: No Laughing Matter," *LeaderPerfect Newsletter*, August 15, 2007 (reprinted with permission), http://www.leaderperfect.com/newsletter/past_issues/aug1507.htm.

5. Anna Freud, *The Ego and the Mechanisms of Defense* (Madison, CT: International Universities Press; Revised edition, June 1967).

5

To Move Mountains You Must First Move People

The difference between mere management and leadership is communication.

Winston Churchill

OUT OF THE FIRE AND INTO THE FRYING PAN

For most entrepreneurs, talking is almost effortless. At times mindless. But real communication—conveying knowledge, feelings, opinions, ideas, or actions to be taken—is not that simple. It is a cultivated art that requires great, mindful skill. As you move at lightning speed throughout your day—going from one task to another, trying to pack it all in as you persuade, interview, sell, negotiate, motivate, and inspire others—typical entrepreneurs may forget that on the other side of their communication is a human being. And these human beings are trudging along, doing their tasks for the day—at times frustrated, anxious, withdrawn, or self-absorbed. So the entrepreneur's job is two-fold—to convey the message and also analyze how that message is being understood.

The Breakdown

How can the think-fast-on-your-feet entrepreneur become a master of communication, first engaging people, and then moving them to action? Here's what happened with Lani, a wannabe entrepreneur graduating from one of the top business schools in the country.

Having studied entrepreneurship, she felt ready to step out on her own. Only Lani did not know that her communication skills were limited.

"I've come from one of the top universities. I have studied all the skills I'll need," was her naïve incantation.

As she set out to start up her own Internet business, she had little overhead. Two years later as she began to expand, so did the expenses. She needed more office space to hire more employees.

As the employee count grew to 10, challenges came up for all. Lani began having difficulty getting her team to work well together. On their own, each member was capable and forthcoming with information; however, as a team, they were disjointed and uncommunicative. At times their inappropriate responses to her directives infuriated her. She felt trapped, not knowing what to do.

Lani's bewilderment and frustration grew, and she continued to blame her employees. The company was losing its direction. Future cohesiveness of her team was threatened. Was the problem really with the employees? Or was it with Lani?

Although a whiz-kid in statistics, accounting, and business management theory, she had no idea that her lack of leadership and interpersonal skills was putting the company in jeopardy.

It was her accountant who suggested she contact me for help.

EFFECTIVE COMMUNICATION BRINGS SUCCESS

I suggested to Lani that she meet with her team once a week and to take notice of the communication that was exchanged. She reported back that she thought people were walking away from these meetings unclear about her long-term vision and not connected to her urgency.

"How do you know that?" I asked her.

Lani replied that they didn't handle customer complaints well, at least not the way she wanted them handled. They seemed not concerned about expenses and wasteful. And they hardly ever met together without her being present.

Through the grapevine, she revealed to me, she had heard that people feared her. At times even Ross, her inventory and warehouse manager and long time friend, spoke about her tyrannical rule and would have liked to dethrone her.

The meetings became a dreaded event, and some employees made excuses not to show up. Lani was confused and couldn't understand her role in all of this.

This was great information for me to begin to coach Lani.

First, Look Inside

Lani's situation demonstrated that true leadership is about understanding yourself first, then using that knowledge to build a great company. Lani's initial task from coaching would be to gain a better understanding of her communication style.

With effective communication comes stronger relationships, which builds trust; the fostering of creativity, which brings innovation and change; alignment of others to her vision; and the achievement of business results, faster and with less stress.

Some business leaders have never looked closely at their communication until a debacle occurs and then they may be forced to do so. Lucky for Lani, she caught the breakdown occurring and would be able to stave off greater disruptions in communication and productivity.

Synchronicity

If she wanted to build a company to flourish long-term, it was to begin with her communication. Then she could coach others to explore their own communication style and synchronize communication amongst all of them.

Just as it takes each rower in a boat to row in harmony to reach their destination with speed and accuracy, so does it also take each member of a team to communicate well amongst themselves to achieve efficient and effective results.

Feedback

I suggested to Lani that we get feedback from her employees to understand some of the problems they faced. She agreed. In response to questions, Lani became clear about their concerns and frustrations. At times, many of them felt she communicated as a dictator, not taking into consideration their task load or what they were currently doing when she'd interrupt them with *something of more importance*.

Some of the employees said that Lani talked down to them, making them feel stupid. She never used the word *stupid*, although she did admit to me that at times when she was most frustrated with an employee; she'd wonder whether they were incompetent.

Most of her team said they were constantly criticized and given little praise. When they'd approach Lani with feedback on her style of communication, she'd deny it and get defensive. At the weekly team meetings, Lani would constantly check her watch as she robotically ran through her agenda. Then she'd expect everyone to understand, agree, and get moving on it. Lani tried to motivate people, but it was apparent she just didn't know how, and instead people became more agitated.

The State of Alignment

Optimum levels of performance can only be achieved with an aligned team—where everyone is working together to create predetermined company results. The entrepreneur must help others to set aside their differences of opinion and judgments in order to achieve the goals. This takes clear and concise communication.

Alignment is an art form, like dance. When both partners are dancing in sync, there is a flow. When communication is flowing, the team is flowing together. When it is closed down, everyone is stepping on each other's feet.

Some yell *ouch* and others drop their head and walk away brooding. The latter describes Lani's team.

Alignment is vital to success, but because it is not tangible—you can't see or touch it like a loaf of bread—it is difficult to know when it isn't present. Yet alignment is as important as the air we breathe. It acts as an invisible cord that connects people to each other. Alignment is not a problem to be solved, but a state to be managed.

I gave Lani the following checklist to better communicate her expectations and the taking of action:

1. Make requests, not demands. Explain why you are making the request and the benefits it will have.
2. Follow through with the appropriate corrective actions where needed.
3. When giving feedback, focus on the behaviors you want to see, not criticisms or judgments. Never attack someone's character or competency.
4. Take responsibility for your communication to be clear and understood.
5. De-personalize defensiveness. Don't react to what you may consider a negative comment pointed at you. Take a step back, take a deep breath and concentrate on the message instead.
6. Trust others before they can prove themselves to you. Expect it and you shall receive it.

AUTHENTIC COMMUNICATION

Authentic communication is about accepting responsibility, aligning messages with core values, goals, mission, or vision; respectful transmission of ideas; always checking assumptions at the door; and being honest.[1]

Leadership communication is effectively motivating, directing, inspiring, and guiding. It is result-oriented and often team-oriented.

Four Styles of Communication

The model for communication styles that I compiled came from my research on Jung's work on personality types: the Thinker, Feeler, Sensor, and Intuitor[2] and William Marston's[3] work on behavior styles.

Personality types or styles date back to Ancient Greece when Hippocrates formulated four styles of temperament according to the four elements: earth, wind, fire, and water.

While each style of communication has its pros and cons, you'll get the best response from others when you incorporate your listener's communication style into your own. To identify their communication style, listen closely and see if you can determine their dominant style. Good communicators will practice combining all of the styles instead of using just one. If there is more than one person with whom you are speaking, then you may want to incorporate a combination of the four styles.

Let's examine the differences between the different styles of communication.

The Includer (or Team Player)

Communicates ...
- With the focus on "Why?"
- Sincerely
- Kindly
- Considerately
- Sympathetically
- Excitedly
- Wanting to forge forward
- With rapport by first speaking about personal interest or events
- With a focus on change that will impact relationships more positively

The Includer Must Learn

Not everyone needs to be included all of the time. They do not need to make everyone feel good.

The Helper (or Expresser)

Communicates ...
- With the focus on "Who?"
- Expressively
- Spiritedly
- Helpfully
- To build relationships
- To avoid rejection and impersonal feelings
- With a focus on the big picture for people and teams
- To give a lot of information; at times, to the point of getting side-tracked. May need extra time to communicate.
- For enjoyment
- To manage conflicts, differences of opinion, and challenges
- Excitedly

The Helper Must Learn

To stay on topic and to stop trying to over-sell their point.

The Thinker (or Systematizer)

Communicates . . .
- With the focus on "How?"
- Technically
- Systematically
- For details and information
- Analytically
- Thoroughly and logically using facts, details, and reasons
- Slowly and deliberately
- First by thinking through things before speaking
- In order to prevent mistakes
- With a focus to avoid change and conflict

The Thinker Must Learn

To move away from all the details and push self into the bigger picture.

The Driver (or Challenger)

Communicates . . .
- With the focus on "What (results will get produced)?"
- Straightforward and boldly
- To get their way
- For competition, wants to win
- Bluntly and aggressively
- Quickly, concisely, and with clarity
- To challenge
- To get fast results
- To make the decisions and avoid someone else making them
- To drive
- With goal-orientation and has expectations that others will also communicate with the focus on goals
- With not strong listening skills

The Driver Must Learn

To hold back on responding quickly and not to cut people off.

BECOME A SKILLED COMMUNICATOR

Here are some important strategies to develop skillful communication:

1. Get crystal clear in your message then deliver it articulately and with clarity. This includes speaking and writing. You can build your skills by reading more each day.
2. Be authentic. Don't try to sound like someone else. Incorporate the communication style of your listener but don't deny your own way of being.
3. Get acknowledgement that your message is understood. Don't leave until you are sure.
4. Live by your words. Walk the talk you speak.
5. Speak with a consciousness of opening up communication. Let go of being defensive and let others get their point across. Don't mock or insult others.
6. Speak from conviction to build trust and confidence. This motivates people to take action. Wavering creates mistrust.
7. Stay positive and look for the positive in others. Criticism and blame destroys trust. Don't exaggerate or distort information.
8. Stay focused on the issue, not personalities or other judgments.
9. If you're angry, state it and move on in a controlled manner, don't walk around brooding and silent. People will misinterpret this and get anxious. Their concern will be on you and the longevity of their career versus their work.
10. Come to a resolution if there is conflict.
11. Know your communication style and that of your listener.

The Turn-around

Lani came to understand that her style was *The Driver*. At first she wanted to deny it. But as we worked together, she came to accept it. Eventually she talked about it and could even laugh at herself. This lightened things up and people stopped fearing her. She was more approachable—more human.

Each person on her team identified their style of communication. With time and practice, they were able to recognize the styles of other people and structure their own communication around the listener's style. This brought a greater level of acceptance.

With Lani's business education and new tools to distinguish and change her communication style, she transformed her team into an aligned, cohesive group.

ASK YOURSELF

The highest reward for a person's toil is not what they get for it, but what they become by it.

John Ruskin

Take some quality time to get quiet, close your eyes, and ask yourself these questions.

1. What is your style of communication?
2. What is the biggest frustration you face today?
3. How does it relate back to your own communication?
4. What are three ways you can change your communication beginning now?
5. Think of someone you have a hard time listening to. What would you like to change about their communication?

PRACTICE THIS

Practice #1: To Get Your Message Across, Become Yourself

Understand your style of communication. Don't change it, just yet. Instead, study it. Learn more about the vocabulary you use, and your different intonations and their usage. How do you deliver bad news? Praise? Reprimands? Are they effective? You'll know by the response you get from others.

If your company is reaching its goals, your team is aligned, and communication is open, you can probably concentrate your efforts elsewhere. But if you're like most entrepreneurs, this is an area for continual work.

Once you understand your style and how it comes across to others, see what elements you can incorporate into it. Don't change your communication. Just include other strategies and styles. Become a better you.

If you are *The Driver*, like Lani, then look at how you can soften your delivery so that people will take the action you need. Look to see what is missing in your communication to really motivate your team. Are you asking them to step up and become leaders or are you always directing them?

Know yourself. Be true to yourself. Then incorporate other elements from other styles to help you become the best you.

Practice #2: Seek to Understand before Being Understood

Listen, listen, then listen some more. People will tell you about how they think, how they feel, and in essence who they are. They may say it in words, but also tell you in nonverbal communication, such as open or closed body language, facial expressions, and tone.

Listening will allow you to really understand the other person's message. Too many times we're so concerned about being understood instead of understanding. We'll fight for the right to be understood. And sometimes while you're fighting to be understood, so is the other person. Then there are two people trying to be understood. When you notice this happening, stop. Begin to really listen. Allow the other person the soap box. That is why we were given two ears and one mouth—to listen more than we speak.

Once the other person feels understood, they'll let go of their tight grip to talk, be right, and to make you wrong. To be understood, first understand.

Practice #3: Make Attitude Your Figure of Speech

Eat lunch in the company lunch room once a week. Create an atmosphere where people can speak freely to you. Gripes are better stated to you, than kept inside—creating gossip and mischief. Communicate openness by walking your talk. This is not about becoming a friend, but a trusted, respected leader.

Practice #4: Remember: If You Win, You Really Lose

Creating an atmosphere for cohesiveness is the key. Communication is the first step. If you bully or threaten people, they may do what you request, but they won't do it because they want to or with their heart in it. They'll do it to save their job. And then without you knowing it, they may do little things to sabotage the company's growth.

When I'm shopping in a store, I might strike up a conversation with the sales associate or manager and ask how they like working at their company.

Too many times they'll shrug their shoulders and tell me, "It's ok, but I'm looking for a better company."

They may even continue on with some complaints about it. It doesn't make for a good shopping experience, nor does it make for good marketing of their company.

Imagine if your employee spoke about the company in that manner. How would that impact your customer? Create your employees to have a voice in what is working and what isn't. Allow them the independence to find solutions to problems they face. Open up the space for them to jump out of their comfort zone, state their gripe, and then encourage them to go fix it. When you do this, you are building a future leader, not just an employee who takes orders.

As you challenge your people, you'll help build their self-esteem and trust. People will walk on water for you if they know you have their best interest at heart. Create a win-win atmosphere at all times.

Practice #5: You Must Trust before You Can Be Trusted

When I was interviewing entrepreneurs for this book, I asked about trust. How do you develop trust in your employees? How do employees learn to trust you?

Mostly everyone I interviewed had an issue with trust. Many got animated and heated as they talked about employees who "screwed" them. But there was one entrepreneur who very softly told me, "Once I hire someone, I don't wait for that person to show me trust. I begin by trusting them. Then guess what? Trust shows up. They begin to trust me. It never fails."

Trust before you have any reason to. Start today. List three ways you can begin to trust your people. You may have to give something up, such as control, but in the long-run it will be well worth it. Then bring these three elements into every interaction for a month. You'll find that it will begin to become a natural part of your communication with others. Trust or the lack of it, can take a company to success or failure.

SUMMARY

☑ Communication impacts alignment and success.
☑ Communication is the key to a company's growth.
☑ Effective communication brings stronger relationships which builds trust, a fostering of innovation and change, and a connection to the company's vision.
☑ There are four styles of communication, the: Includer, Helper, Thinker, and Driver.
☑ Know your communication style. Don't try to change it entirely. Don't incorporate other styles into it.
☑ Get to know your employees. Have lunch with them weekly.
☑ To be understood, first understand.
☑ Become a trusted, respected leader by listening to gripes.
☑ Build independence and self esteem by encouraging employees to go ahead and find a solution to their gripe.
☑ Create a win-win atmosphere.
☑ Trust employees before you have any reason to.

NOTES

1. J. LaCosta, BlueRio Strategies, PowerPoint presentation, 2008.
2. Carl Jung, *Psychological Types: The Collected Works of C. G. Jung*, Vol. 6 (Princeton, NJ: Princeton University Press, 1976).
3. William Martston, *Emotions of Normal People* (Cooper Press, 2007).

6

Speak Only Half as Much as You Listen

Of all the skills of leadership, listening is the most valuable, and one of the least understood. Most captains of industry listen only sometimes, and they remain ordinary leaders. But a few, the great ones, never stop listening. That's how they get word before anyone else of unseen problems and opportunities.

Peter Nulty

MARK

Mark was frustrated with his boss' lack of consideration for others. Ted, the boss, allowed the managers in his fast food chain great freedom to make decisions. However, if they needed to speak to him about a matter of concern or just wanted to toss around some ideas, within in seconds Ted was off and running—talking instead of listening. Mark, who was hired three years ago as the marketing guy to help the company grow exponentially, was beginning to feel undervalued. He also knew that Ted would deny that he had any role in Mark's feeling this way.

Hiring Mark

Mark was trained on Madison Avenue. As an account executive, he had been part of a team working with million dollar consumer product accounts at a large advertising firm. He was burned out from stress and his daily commute into New York City each day. When his youngest son entered his senior year of college, he made a promise to take a pay cut and move out of the Big Apple. He kept his promise.

Mark was hired as a marketing manager working for Ted, who owned a chain of fast food restaurants. Ted used outside vendors for his marketing needs, but as his chain of restaurants grew, he needed to bring someone inside. When Ted was introduced to Mark, he knew that he couldn't let someone with his expertise get away. Mark liked Ted's laid back style of management and thought he could help him build an empire.

The company brought in annual revenues of $50 million a year and continued to grow. Mark was impressed by the growth and Ted's emphasis on customer service. The deal was made and even though Ted had recently lost two key people in his media department, Mark thought he could help put a strong marketing team together.

TED

As for Ted, he had been groomed in the restaurant business. His parents and uncles all owned restaurants. During school years he bussed, served, managed, and even worked in the kitchen. He knew early on he would have his own restaurant one day. Upon graduating from Cornell University with a degree in hospitality, he went to work for his father's brother who had a chain of diners. He managed the chain, and under his watch, it began to grow for the first time in a long while.

After several years of socking away his paycheck, Ted was ready to start up his own restaurant.

Growth

It began as a local coffee shop which expanded into lunch, then a bakery was added, and eventually it became a sit down for all three meals. The food was good and word spread quickly. In the morning the smell of freshly baked breads and pastry whiffed through the air, and people lined up at the door. Soon Ted opened up another restaurant on the other side of town, following that with fourteen additional restaurants and five more bakeries. He hired managers and shift supervisors for each location. He currently had a senior team of direct reports from operations, finance, technology, and now marketing.

The Hole in the Dam

Ted's style of management was approachable, and he was everybody's friend. He told great jokes and could keep the staff rolling in laughter from his stories. The customers found him friendly and entertaining.

About one year after Ted had hired Mark, a manager quit. Six months later, another manager quit. Mark knew why, but Ted didn't. Mark didn't see it coming. He could kick himself now for missing it. Looking back at his own interview, he remembered how he felt even then when Ted cut him off mid-sentence. He forgot that it started the moment he met Ted.

Mark should have known in the instant Ted interrupted him, that this was not a trait for building strong relationships. He did not heed Oprah Winfrey's strong advice regarding the importance of first impressions. She states, "When people show you who they are, believe them the first time."[1] But he liked the company and wanted the job. As time went by, perhaps Mark could have continued to tolerate being cut off, but there was another important factor at play here. Ted never listened—he only pretended to.

Oprah Winfrey says, "When you are mistreated the first time, when you see someone who shows you a lack of integrity or dishonesty the first time, know that that will be followed by many, many, many other times that will at some point in life come back to haunt or hurt you. When people show you who they are, believe them, the first time. Live your life from truth and you will survive everything, everything, I believe even death."[2]

Upon first meeting the friendly Ted, people took a liking to him. But if they worked with him side-by-side, day after day, they realized that the relationship was one-sided. Ted loved to talk and he hated to listen. Always in the spotlight as an only child, he was used to the attention. He never had to share the stage with another sibling. As friendships were built, others were lost. He was difficult to tolerate for very long.

Mark was sure that the combination of cutting people off and not listening to much of what they had to say was why Ted was losing some good people.

CONSCIOUS LISTENING

Facing the Issue

When Mark approached Ted to discuss the issue, Ted dismissed him with small talk while shrugging his shoulders. He couldn't understand why the two managers had left and quite frankly didn't really want to understand. At dinner one night, Ted told Mark that if he didn't get some coaching, he would be the next to leave. It was then that Ted stopped talking. He put down his fork, sat back in his chair and had a child-like look of surprise and sadness on his olive-complexioned face.

Ted knew Mark was an asset to the company. He had helped with its recent surge in growth, designing new ads and menu options. He knew many people in the media and called upon them for publicity favors during a grand opening or company event. He was building a quality team who worked well together. Ted realized that he had to take Mark's comment seriously or else he'd lose him too.

Using Three Senses

The good news for Ted and for all of us is that *listening* is a learned skill. The ability to listen is not inherent. This means you can learn how to listen better at any age. Although listening seems like it should be simple, it takes practice and great patience.

Good listening skills require the use of other senses, especially sight and your sixth sense, intuition. Sight allows us to read body language, which is a nonverbal way that we all communicate. For instance, if you tell someone that you're happy to see them but your arms are crossed in front of your chest, the likelihood is that you're closed off to this person in some manner.

Intuition gives us a reality check while using gut reaction. It's a feeling inside. It may be a whisper, bells and whistles going off inside, or a stirring in your stomach. If you're tuned in, you can use your gut as a trusted guide. It will send messages, such as, *is this person telling the truth, or am I safe here?*

Coaching with Ted

Ted took Mark's advice and set up a meeting with me over the phone. Soon after, I began the process of helping him to improve his listening.

When I first began to coach Ted, he constantly interrupted me. A coaching relationship is a microcosm of what is happening on the outside. What is brought to the coaching table is more than likely happening in other places also.

As Ted kept interrupting me, I found that he was also interrupting his employees. Because the employees had never been in coaching, they didn't know that Ted's behavior had little to do with them.

Common to most people who feel they are being ignored, is taking someone's inability to listen personally. You may personalize it with thoughts such as, *I'm not smart enough, he isn't interested in what I say, or who am I to be suggesting something to the boss?*

But this was more about Ted's inability to listen. He didn't realize that when he didn't engage with people, they felt rejected and cut off from him. After a while, his managers stopped coming to him. They complained that they didn't feel like they had anything important to offer him. It's a strong warning sign when your employees stop approaching you. They are your lifeline to your customers and to new business.

Ted had to learn how to listen in a way he had never done before, and he'd have to do it quickly before more managers exited.

Clarity of the Speaker

The ability to listen is dependent on many factors. One is the quality of the message being delivered by the speaker. Although we can't control how a message is being communicated to us, we can become aware that it may not always get delivered in a receivable manner. The following are obstacles that may block your listening.

- Quality of the speaker's voice—volume too loud or too soft.
- Speaker has an accent or uses improper English.
- Complexity of the message—too much information or too many problems stated.
- Nonverbal communication: body language is contrary to the verbal message (e.g., communicator says with crossed arms and a furrowed brow, "I really like your idea").
- Getting lost in the delivery of the story or forgetting the point.

(continued)

- Too sensitive to how the listener is taking the message, or how the listener might react (walking on eggshells).
- Talking in jargon, such as technicians, doctors, or lawyers tend to do.

How We Listen

Other factors that block our listening include the following:

- Already know or assume what the speaker is saying or going to say.
- Lost in your own thoughts about something that you have to do or something that happened.
- Assessments, preconceived thoughts and judgments about what is being said.
- Assessments, preconceived thoughts and judgments about the speaker.
- Looking for an opening to speak.
- Selective hearing, hearing only what you want to hear.
- Preparing what you're going to say next, to suit your needs, not the speaker's.
- Preparing a rebuttal to what is being said.
- Not understanding the speaker and not asking for clarification.
- Hurrying them by looking at your watch, packing up your things to leave, or just wishing they would stop talking because you're in a time crunch or you have more important things to do.
- Remembering your own experience (and daydreaming) similar to the speaker's communicated experience and missing not only what they are saying, but the emotion behind it.
- Discounting what the speaker is saying.
- Yes-ing the speaker—agreeing with what the speaker says to avoid a disagreement or to be nice; promising to do something and knowing that you won't.

Ted's high energy moved him like a race horse throughout his day. He went from internal meetings to outside appointments and business engagements. There was very little flex time in his crammed calendar—least of all, time for a conversation with a complaining employee. If Ted could outrun them, maybe the issues would take care of themselves.

As a goal-driven, time-strapped, results-oriented individual who constantly resisted and eluded distractions and diversions, Ted had to develop into a listener who consciously listened and responded to the needs of employees—time after time.

Ted, with the fierce independence and multi-tasking ability of an entrepreneur, had to learn to shift gears from moving at top speed, and sometimes stepping over or around people, to slow motion. He realized that conscious listening requires attending to an employee's overriding needs of the moment which can impede his own pressing interests. *Becoming present* was key to slowing down and listening.

ASK YOURSELF

The following questions will help you to look at your listening. Take some quality time to get quiet, close your eyes, and ask yourself these questions.

1. When a deadline is looming and someone comes into my office to talk to me, what do I do?
2. When someone tells me a story, do I usually respond with something similar that happened to me?
3. When someone comes to me with a problem, do I give feedback or try to solve the problem?
4. Has anyone ever told me that I'm not listening?
5. Have I recognized when someone isn't listening to me?
6. How do I feel when someone is pretending to listen to me?
7. What is one step that I can take immediately to improve my listening?

PRACTICE THIS

Skilled listening is not a passive process of just hearing words. To listen actively, you must be engaged in the communication between the speaker and you. You are listening from the perspective of the speaker, seeing the world through his eyes. This doesn't mean that you have to agree with him, but it is important to listen from his viewpoint.

Misinterpretation of the communication occurs when the listener assumes that they understand what the speaker is saying without getting clarification.

The following are five effective practices to conscious listening that have proven to be successful with Ted and scores of other entrepreneurs with a listening *disability*.

Practice #1: Listen with Your Ears and Your Heart

As business owners and leaders, we move at lightning speed in the desperate state to get it all done—as if we actually ever will. If someone distracts you from what you're doing, especially if you're on a deadline, it's difficult to stop and listen. You may just tune them out and turn them off. But if you knew that listening to them may just make your own tasks easier, wouldn't you begin to listen differently?

Imagine this, you're sitting at your desk and in walks your assistant with a question about a particular caller. You're in the middle of a deadline and begin to tell yourself how ridiculous this is that you must take your precious time to answer her. She's not sure if you want to be interrupted with this caller.

When you inquire, you find out that this caller is an investor who is looking to help fund your next project. It is an important call and one that you forgot to tell your assistant to expect. Instead of berating her silently, you praise her. Lucky for you that she took the time to interrupt you.

Suppose most people just want clarification or someone to listen to them. When you're consciously listening to the person with all three senses: hearing, seeing, and intuition—you are present. When you are present, you have slowed down and can really hear what is being said. Your heart may even open up to the communicator's message. Perhaps you can stand in their shoes and see the world through their eyes. That is an empathic listener. Now suppose that was all you needed to do—nothing to solve, nothing else to do. Just listen.

The following are steps to practice conscious listening:

1. First, agree upon a mutual time to get together.
2. Put aside your judgments and criticisms about this person.
3. Listen to the whole person: hear their words and watch their posture and body language. Listen for the emotion beneath the words.
4. Get in their shoes. How does the world look from their viewpoint?
5. Empathize with their situation. Tell them you really *get it*. This does not mean you are necessarily agreeing; it does means that you hear what they are saying.
6. Feedback what you heard in your own words.
7. Ask them what else they may need at this point in time.
8. Ask them what they are taking away from this conversation.

Practice #2: When You Have the Urge, Bite Your Tongue

When someone is upset and expresses hurt or anger toward you, the first response is usually to defend. Don't. Instead bite your tongue, grip your fist under the desk, or count to 10 silently if need be. Compose yourself. Two upset people attacking each other make matters worse. Instead adopt active listening. Decide whether this is the right time to talk, and if it isn't, choose a mutually agreed upon time to get back together.

Listen to the words and the emotions being communicated. Feed back what you are hearing, but not word for word. This could anger the other person even more because they may think you're mimicking them.

Get clarification. Ask the speaker if what you heard is correct. Then ask them if there is anything more they'd like to say.

Stay calm. Remember, anger wants company. Your role is to remain calm. Be the rock in the relationship for this conversation. Rise above it. No matter what buttons get pushed, keep listening underneath the words for the hurt and pain in the communicator.

Keep asking the communicator if there is anything else they need to say until they are complete.

Be empathic. You can listen to the other person, and be non-judgmental and respectful without invalidating your own point of view.

Acknowledgment of their perspective does not mean you agree, more importantly it means that you have heard them. I believe that is what we want most in this world—to be heard.

Practice #3: Listen for What Isn't Being Said

Listening to the words of the speaker is only part of his communication. Some studies claim that verbal communication is only 7 to 10 percent of what is being communicated. The remainder is in body language and tone of voice.

As the communicator speaks, you will hear the words. Go deeper in your listening. Don't respond right away. Take yourself through the active listening process in Practice #1. Listen to their tone and emotions and for what isn't being said. What do you hear? Sadness? Hurt? Insecurity? To get the speaker to communicate what isn't being said, ask:

1. How did that make you feel?
2. What did you do about it?
3. What would you like to do about it?
4. How would that then feel?
5. Is there anything else you'd like to add to what you've said?

Practice #4: Fight Distractions

When you have agreed upon a time and place to speak, avoid distractions. If you're going to have a difficult conversation, don't meet in a populated place. Instead meet in your office with a posted *Do Not Disturb* sign on the door.

If you keep the door open, avoid high-trafficked times to meet. People walking by, phones ringing, external noises take away from concentration that you, the listener, will have to bring to the conversation.

Think ahead. Is this the right time for you to talk? Can you clear your own mind to be in this conversation? If not, what can you do to clear it? Take a walk? Meditate for two minutes?

Do something that will not only clear external, but also internal distractions.

If the timing isn't right for the conversation, set up another time when you know you can be mentally present.

Practice #5: Listen On-Purpose

Conscious listening is a real art. It is not something that is taught in the classroom or even at the dinner table. When I was growing up, the family member who spoke the loudest at the dining room table, got the floor. In business, that should never be the case.

Listening is a learned skill. It takes concentration, intention, clear-headedness, and commitment. As a leader, active listening should be one of the 10 commandments of leadership and should be included in all business school curriculums.

Read books on listening, practice with your children and your partner or spouse. They will be your toughest and most honest critics if you instruct them to critique your listening.

To listen consciously—on purpose, you must bring yourself into the moment. If you are thinking about a problem or something that must be done, you have compromised your listening.

The more skilled a listener you become, the more you will learn. As you learn more, you become a more empathic and better leader and human being.

Keen listening skills will catapult an entrepreneur to unlimited success in areas that are essential to personal and business growth.

SUMMARY

- ☑ Listening includes three senses: hearing, seeing, and intuition.
- ☑ Delivery of the message, including voice, jargon, body language, and clarity of the speaker can impact listening.
- ☑ Assessments, judgments, and preconceived thoughts impact listening.
- ☑ To listen actively, you must be engaged in the communication between the speaker and yourself.
- ☑ Always get clarification.
- ☑ When listening, be present.
- ☑ Conscious listening is with intention, on-purpose, or deliberately, just as if you were doing some other task.
- ☑ Listen for what isn't being said.
- ☑ What we want most is to be heard.
- ☑ Limit distractions.

NOTES

1. Oprah Winfrey, Commencement Address, Wellesley College, May 30, 1997.
2. Ibid.

7

Get to Know Your Top Advisor—You

Your vision will become clear only when you look into your heart. Who looks outside, dreams. Who looks inside, awakens.

Carl Jung

Elliot took a leap. At the time, it was a very painful leap—not the type entrepreneurs want to take. To most, he was living the dream life. People who never owned a business couldn't understand why he did it. People who owned a business didn't want to look too closely at what he did, as if it could happen to them. But for Elliot, it was the only option.

THE MAKING AND BREAKING OF AN ENTREPRENEUR

It was five years since he had started the company that grew to $2.5 million in annual revenues. Never receiving a college degree, he had worked for several small business owners during high school. After graduation, he answered phones for an IT company in Texas. The manager saw raw talent in Elliot and wisely promoted him to other roles. The company was eventually sold to an IT outsourcing firm and Elliot stayed with the new owners. They sent him to technical classes and he developed a strong working knowledge of software development. He excelled both in his studies and with the working knowledge he brought to the company.

Prompted by some nagging desire to do better and a restlessness deep inside, he started up his own software solutions business. Keeping his day job as he started this company was quite a juggling act for Elliot. When the revenue started to flow, he devoted full time to it. The company grew rapidly and went from a solo-entrepreneurship to a full fledged company with 20 employees. Elliot's life was consumed with the growth of his business, and outside of some time spent with his twin sons and wife, he dedicated his days to the company. Besides his business was fun. He was doing what he wanted to do. It couldn't get any better than this.

Sales grew rapidly. Elliot made the deadly mistake of not keeping a watchful eye on expenses. He was not skilled in the area of profit and loss but sales were pouring in, so he figured, why worry?

The Downturn

Then it happened. The company's growth stalled. It was as if it was finally catching up with itself from the *out of the gate* speed of early growth. Elliot certainly was not prepared. Inexperienced at growing a company and not geared up for the slow down in sales, he turned to advisors who gave him guidance, especially to tighten up on spending. Yet, he ignored their counsel. Elliot had a good reserve of cash and a strong line of credit that could hold them for a few months. He was confident that the company would come out of this tailspin soon.

The managers who reported to Elliot looked to him for any cues of concern. None came. Business as usual was still the call.

Elliot prided himself as a technician—a software builder. His leadership of people and management of functions were limited and it began to show when sales slowed down. Hiring too many of the wrong people within a short period of time had a damaging impact. It cost money to hire, train, and fire someone; then to do it all over again. This didn't happen once or twice, it was a continual turnstile.

Confidence dropped. Concern surfaced. Service suffered and customers complained. Employees worked overtime and didn't feel appreciated. Elliot struggled to turn the company around. Life as an entrepreneur with double digit profits was over. He had watched his father go bankrupt and fear invaded every cell of Elliot's body.

The End in Sight

Every month-end, when profit and loss was calculated, Elliot's world whirled around. He held his breath waiting to see if he would have enough money to pay bills, employee salaries, taxes, benefits, and himself. Most recently the numbers took him to the edge. He was just making it, but with little breathing room. He knew they couldn't last like this for very long. Each month he dipped further into his own savings to pull the company out. The inevitable grew near.

Home life was already stressful even without the decline of his business. The twins were just two months old. Jamie, his wife, had stopped working to raise their sons, so he was the sole income provider. He cut back his salary to help keep the business running. Sleep eluded him with nighttime feedings of the twins. The loneliness grew darker in the wee hours of the morning even as he held his babies in his arms. He began to look at them as burdens, not a source of joy.

Middle of the Night Decision

As the fifth anniversary of the company approached and with sales down and the economy failing, he had to reinvent the way they did business or get out. He was tired, confused, and panicked. Pent up fear consumed him; he didn't talk to anyone about his feelings. He suffered like this for months.

One night Elliot snapped out of sleep and sat up. Had he been dreaming or just surface sleeping and thinking as he waited for the babies to cry? His face was wet as if he had been weeping in his sleep.

It was the first time in months that he had clarity about his situation. He knew what he was going to do. The verdict was made in his sleep. This did not bring him solace.

For three days he sat with his decision, not speaking to anyone about it. What he was about to do would be a near impossible task. Elliot spoke to his accountant and some close business friends. All advised him not to do it. Then on day four, he met with a colleague whom he respected. Although Elliot knew his direction, it was important for at least one person (he trusted) to understand and confirm his decision.

The colleague listened carefully to Elliot over two cups of coffee, asked good questions, and then said, "Alright."

He was in agreement. As if by osmosis, Elliot felt his load lighten. He came out of paralysis and into action. Elliot was going to retire the business.

Trust Your Inner Voice

Elliot knew deep inside the moment it was done. He knew the split second he felt that he couldn't spend another day in the business. The downturn was ripping him apart. It felt out of his control. To fix it would take great effort—more than he was able to exert. He was tired. No, exhausted. In fact, Elliot sensed that additional effort to fix his business would just about kill him, as harsh as that sounded. His mother had died of a heart attack when he was 20. If stress continued to consume him, he would follow in her footsteps.

Elliot's mother left him an invaluable gift—a message.

She always told him, "Trust your gut, it will never steer you wrong."

This advice helped Elliot through school and business. Later on it was this advice that helped him to open the door into marriage with a woman he loved. During the five years of running his business, he also relied on that inner voice to help guide him through tough decisions, whether firing someone or investing in a big ticket item to support growth.

During this whole period of time, he could hear his inner guidance system telling him, "Get out from under this burden of a business I have to bear. I'll be alright. I have done well. It was now time to move on."

But he wanted to ignore it.

Your Top Advisor

Closing a business is monumental. The physical strength required is huge, the mental strength even greater.

Elliot now had to have a conversation with Jamie. She cried in his arms while each held a baby. They were scared. What was going to happen to all of them? Elliot explained that there was no choice. Even if he tried to sell the business in this economy, it would take time—more time than they had. The bills could wipe out their entire personal savings. They could lose their home. Jamie blamed his advisors, the economy, and vendors who she felt were ripping Elliot off. She even blamed the customers.

When disaster strikes and emotions run high, hope can get lost. It happened to Elliot and Jamie. Not only were they losing a business and an income, but also their future. Everything they had dreamed about—more children, Jamie staying home to raise the kids, vacations, college funds, and the good life of fortune was going down the toilet. The babies' cries were now mixed with Jamie's. And late at night in the privacy of his personal space, Elliot joined them.

The Toll

Elliot made arrangements to close his company. It had to be done quickly because he didn't have the money to continue to fund it. With the advice of an attorney, he packed up the office with the help of his father and three brothers. A used furniture company gave him a token amount of what he had paid for the office furniture. He notified employees who were stunned, but later would say they saw it coming. He delivered written notice to the realty company and called the vendors asking for longer terms to pay past due bills.

For reasons that didn't make much sense to him, legal actions were taken against Elliot and the company. The swiftness of his decision made customers angry. He would continue to honor and complete all contracts. Even though he personally called customers to let them know the company was closing and that he would still fulfill on his commitment, some angrily dismissed him. Others sent him blessings of good luck. Elliot wondered why it was that in times of misfortune, there were some people who would empathize and others who would use it to their advantage.

His fear elevated to paranoia. Elliot rarely left the house unless he had to go somewhere. He feared he'd run into someone he knew—a previous customer, an employee, or just someone who'd ask how things were going. He was embarrassed and guilt-ridden. Deep shame at what he had caused others, pervaded every cell in his body. He took the full weight of his deeds on his back and it showed. The burden was probably subconscious penance for his poor planning and judgment.

Eventually Elliot was forced to file bankruptcy. The world around him finally quieted down. Now he could step back, and decide what he was going to do next.

FROM FAILURE

Most entrepreneurs view failure as the enemy that stops us on our charted course. And yes, it does stop us, at least for a bit. Failure's greatest gift, however, is that it brings a brilliant reminder telling us to stop and reassess. We may never do that if it weren't for our failures.

J. K. Rowling, famed author of the Harry Potter series, gave the 2008 commencement speech to Harvard University graduates. She spoke about her years before her success, when her failure followed her everywhere. Rowling got great value from that period of time in her life.

On Failure

Rowling states that failure is a gift that shows us who we truly are, and that without it, we would never know our real strengths.

> Failure meant a stripping away of the inessential. I stopped pretending to myself that I was anything other than what I was ... And so rock bottom became the solid foundation on which I rebuilt my life.
>
> It is impossible to live without failing at something, unless you live so cautiously that you might as well not have lived at all—in which case, you fail by default.
>
> Failure gave me an inner security ... Failure taught me things about myself that I could have learned no other way. I discovered that I had a strong will, and more discipline than I had suspected ... The knowledge that you have emerged wiser and stronger from setbacks means that you are, ever after, secure in your ability to survive. You will never truly know yourself, or the strength of your relationships, until both have been tested by adversity. Such knowledge is a true gift; for all that it is painfully won.[1]

The Aftermath

Elliot's hell only lasted 6 months. During that time, he didn't know if he would make it out alive. Paying attention to his inner voice took time and patience.

Wanting to deny what he knew he had to do was a typical first reaction. But because Elliot was attuned to this voice from past practice, he came to rely on it like a trusted friend. The depth of this decision had so many ramifications that the noise in his head—the worry, guilt, doubt, and fear—tried to block out his deep routed guidance system. With no plans for the future in mind, no income, very confused employees, upset clients, and deep depression and anxiety, he added a new partner to this mix—shame. He questioned his decision for months after. Had he made the right decision?

THE INNER VOICE OF WISDOM

Ironically, looking back six years later, he wouldn't have done it any other way. He couldn't have. In fact, today he tells people it was the best decision he has ever made. He gained freedom, but the cost was great. Nonetheless, he knew the route he took was not for the faint of heart.

Sometimes this inner voice, our sixth sense or intuition, indicates what we can't see through human thought or vision.

It takes real courage at times to listen to our internal voice.

There is no flashing neon arrow at the crossroad pointing to the right answers when making a tough decision. Elliot couldn't understand in the moment why his inner voice was leading him to take such a large leap of faith—closing a business without something else to move into. Years later, Elliot opened up another software company that exploded in growth. This time he was prepared for the next recession as he closely watched expenses and stayed within a strict budget.

Because he had listened to his top advisor, that inner voice, he opened the door to a future he'd never regret and a successful new business.

Celebrate Failure

Failure comes in degrees. Elliot's closing of his business was on the extreme.

Strangely enough failure of any degree can give us an opportunity to celebrate. I'm not talking about celebration in the way most people think of it. It's not all the hoopla that's made when you close a long-awaited deal, or when a key employee is won over to your company from the competition. It's not even about festive moments when an entrepreneur sells the company and realizes a windfall.

This type of celebration comes from falling down—hard. The ability to celebrate at this moment is the true mark of a courageous and reflective leader. And it's something more, as well: celebration opens the pathway for your authenticity to shine through. You are seen as real, not the person who doesn't make mistakes or is on a pedestal. This is truly important to people such as your team, your children, and your peers. As you let your failures be seen, you allow for others to acknowledge their failures too. They too then can grab the gifts failure brings.

Ok, we all know that it's easy to celebrate when you're on top of the world, having just scored another victory. But it's darn hard, as it was for Elliot, to celebrate when you've been defeated. Yet this is just the time to do so.

Let's say that you lost out on the biggest contract of your career—or that your top salesperson, who you believed would stay with you forever, just gave notice. Most entrepreneurs when hit from behind will stumble and fall, trying hard to get back into action as soon as possible. There's no time to waste. They swiftly put aside what just happened by assuming automatic behavior patterns—working harder, perhaps eating more, avoiding communication with others, turning to whatever happens to be the usual method for escape. But I'm asking you to imagine what would happen if, when hard times strike, you fall and *don't* rush to get right up. Some might call this— breaking from the usual routine. Seeing with new eyes, you turn adversity into a lesson, which in turn, becomes a celebration of who you are becoming.

Failure is not something to be shameful of, but something to hold, like a cherished memento. It may be our biggest teacher.

ASK YOURSELF

Take some quality time to get quiet, close your eyes, and ask yourself these questions. Mull over these questions for awhile before you answer them. It's fine to ask the question in your mind and then go about your day, with the questions in the background. Sometimes answers come to me best this way—when I'm in the middle of doing something, anything, but thinking about the questions I'm asking myself. It's more fun this way because I don't have to press for answers; they just seem to appear.

1. What is the most public and/or embarrassing failure you've ever had?
2. How did you respond to it?
3. When the dust settled, how did it all turn out—what was the outcome?
4. What did you learn? How would you do it differently next time?
5. How have you incorporated those lessons into your life and work today?

PRACTICE THIS

Now that you've asked and answered the questions in the Ask Yourself section, you're ready to take on the following practices. You may want to read these practices all at once, one a day, or one a week.

Post the practice where it is visible—on your computer, desk, nightstand, console in your car, mirror, and/or refrigerator. Read it once in the morning and once in the evening. Really read it. Take the time to let it absorb. Don't read it to just check it off your to-do list. Commit to practicing it each day.

In the beginning, you'll have to remind yourself of the practice during the day, but as you apply them they will become part of your routine, part of you.

These practices will help you to meet defeat, instead of running from it. You'll uncover the hidden gift beneath the darkness of failure: to have success, you must experience and learn from failure.

Practice #1: When You Fall Down, Stay There Awhile

Our biggest leaps seem to always come from failure and great pain. When failure of any scale occurs, stop what you're doing—even if the pause is short-lived.

The path to personal growth and fulfillment is one filled with many twists and turns. Just when you think you're beyond it all, the next door slams shut on your progress. You can either ram your way through it or stop and take some time to observe it. In the moment of it's occurring it may be impossible to observe. The human tendency is to try and resist it, or push past pain and leave it behind as fast as possible. But growth comes from these barriers. When you're nose to nose with a challenge that has the potential for failure, the first step is to stop what you're doing. Notice that something has happened to take you off course, no matter how large or small. Get in touch with your frustration, disappointment, even the pain. Can you feel where it is at in your body? Is it in your chest? Is it hard to breathe? Maybe it's in your stomach, turning and twisting it with great pressure. Or possibly you feel in it your face as your jaw tightens and your eyes get scrunched. Just notice where it is impacting you physically.

As hard as it may be, resist moving forward right away. You have just opened up an important door. You're at a crossroads. There are two signs. Be sure that you take the road that says *Slow Down*, not the one that says *Keep Moving Fast*.

Imagine that at the end of the *Slow Down* road is a gift wrapped in colorful paper with a big bright bow. It's a special gift with your name on it; one that you can only have if you stop to acknowledge that something just happened to take you off course. You may not know what really occurred, and that is okay for right now. There is nothing else to do in this practice, but to stop, notice the feelings evoked and the impact is has on you physically. Do a body scan. This is also a great practice when you face trauma of any degree.

Practice #2: Write It Down

When something goes wrong, what do you say? Are you aware that you're blaming yourself or others? Do you begin to doubt your decisions? Then this is a good time to get out of your head. By that I mean . . . stop the jabbering inside.

The best way to do this is to write down your thoughts. If you're an extrovert like me, you may prefer to talk through your problems with another person. But writing has a great advantage. It always seems to help me determine, or get clarity on, what just happened. You don't have to have perfect spelling or grammar. You can curse and make nasty wishes on the person who did you wrong. It's good to get the anger out. Writing is harmless and helpful. You can write in incomplete sentences. Punctuation isn't required. This is for your eyes only. This is a place for you to vent.

Perhaps you'll read what you've written at a later date, or never give it another glance. Sometimes I'll write something and then crumble it up and throw it away. If you want, you can even shred it. I've known some people to write out their feelings about a difficult incident and then take a lighter to it, letting it burn in their sink. Before they set it on fire, they ask forgiveness for the pain they've caused, or they'll give forgiveness to those who've cause them pain. The burning is symbolic of letting it go.

The purpose of this practice is to get out of your head and onto paper what happened to cause you such pain. Think of it as turning on the faucet and letting your thoughts flow in no perfect order. Whatever you write will be fine. There's only one requirement. Just be honest.

I would suggest that you get a notebook or journal. That way you can keep all of your writing together in a bound book, should you choose to hold onto it. I prefer a smaller notebook, one that I can throw in my purse or briefcase and carry with me to capture my thoughts at any time.

In your writing tell about the event that caused you to feel sad, angry, or frustrated. I've included the following statements to help you get started.

The thought of what happened makes me feel _____.
If only I could have seen this coming, I would have_____.
Out of nowhere, this came and hit me from behind. It all happened _____.
I'm so angry at _____ I could _____.
This would never have happened, if _____.
I can't believe how _____ they were.
If I ever run into him again, I'll _____.

Practice #3: Find the Higher Meaning

Because you have taken time to stop, do an internal check on your emotions and body, and record your thoughts, you are ready to go beyond the chaos and find new meaning to what happened.

When you look at the incident from far above, and not at ground zero, you'll have better insight to the situation. For this practice, I'm asking you to take a look from 500 feet above.

Here's an example of what I mean. Envision a bird flying hundreds of feet above you. Its perspective is different than yours on ground level. Consider yourself like a Whooper Swan during migration. Whooper Swans have been seen on radar over Northern Ireland at 29,000 feet. (Now that's a bird's eye view!)[2]

At ground zero you can only see so far. At 500 feet above you'll take more into your focus. At 29,000 feet you'll get an entirely different perspective. For example, at ground level you can see the forest on fire. At 500 feet above, you can see the people playing with matches, scared and running away. At 29,000 feet you can see the entrance roads to bring the fire engines into the forest. Higher up gives you more access to answers.

Ask yourself, "What do I need to learn here? What is a different path or course of action I will take the next time this happens?"

Here are some possible responses to those questions:

Compassion for self
Compassion for others
Trust in self
Trusting others
Faith that it will always work out

(continued)

A feeling of deserving (to have)
Self-nurturing
Not putting myself second
Choosing what's right for me

Remember what Rowling said, "It is impossible to live without failing at something, unless you live so cautiously that you might as well not have lived at all—in which case, you fail by default."

Practice #4: When It Is Time, Get Back Up

You will know when it is time to get back up. Trust that you are about to grow—to learn something new. Although the gift or lesson may not appear immediately, it's on its way. Stay open and observant. It may come in small ways. All of a sudden a deal you've been waiting for closes, or you hear good news, find money, or meet a new friend.

Listen and watch for clues that may be very subtle. Trust that these clues will help you move forward in the perfect direction.

Practice #5: Celebrate the Gift from Failure

Even if you don't feel like celebrating, do it anyway. If you've completed the first four practices, you're now ready for the final practice—*change your outlook.*

Instead of seeing the failure, look for the gift. Know that this gift will bring you future success and it was a necessary step in order to get you to where you want to go. That is surely reason to celebrate.

So go on now and celebrate your failure—celebrate it as a way to honor yourself. You can do this by planning something soulful such as a stroll on the beach, a walk in nature, listening to inspiring music, meditating or yoga, and being kind to yourself.

When it looks like its just one thing after another that's coming at you, think of it as one gift after another. I know that isn't how you'll first experience it. But with practice you will. Next time you fail—celebrate.

Great leaders have met with defeat many times and forcefully pushed it behind them. But the gifted leader meets failure, honors it, and then celebrates it knowing that there is a hidden gift beneath the darkness of defeat.

SUMMARY

☑ Failure is not something to be shameful of, but something to hold. It is our biggest teacher.

☑ Human tendency is to push quickly through failure and pain.

☑ Instead, become aware that something has taken you off course, then stop and do nothing.

☑ See the new landscape by journaling your thoughts about the failure or pain.
☑ Find the higher reason for why this breakdown happened.
☑ Honor yourself by taking walks, listening to music, and being kind to yourself.
☑ Look for the gift or lesson in failure; then celebrate it, instead of pushing it away.
☑ Failure of any size is your ally, not your enemy—embrace it.

NOTES

1. J. K. Rowling, "The Fringe Benefits of Failure, and the Importance of Imagination," Harvard University Commencement Address, June 5, 2008.

2. Paul Ehrlich, David Dobkin, and Darryl Wheye, *The Birder's Handbook, A Field Guide to the Natural History of North American Birds* (New York: Fireside, 1988), 83.

8

Be Accountable

No snowflake in an avalanche ever feels responsible.

Stanislaw Lec

GOING PUBLIC

Dropping out of college, David cut his teeth in business working for his father's friend, Alan, who owned a chain of appliance stores. He found his way in business driving delivery trucks and stocking shelves in the warehouse. Eventually he became the chief operating officer.

After Alan's heart attack at the age of 50, David was the likely successor to take over the reins of the 22 stores with annual gross revenue of $30 million, and a half million in profit. Within five years time, he bought Alan out. At the age of 32, David had expanded the chain to 30 stores, and thinking ahead, added environmentally green, solar and wind products. He also set up an Internet marketing business to sell the company products. Sales sky-rocketed. They literally "went off the charts," David claimed. The $30 million company was now a $70 million company with profits touching $5 million.

David wanted more. He dreamt about the day he would take the company public, despite Alan's strong preference not to do so. Alan didn't put it in writing, but requested that David keep it *family-owned*. Taking it public would change that image. Still David knew the direction he was going in and hired Howard, an initial public offering (IPO) consultant to help. Over the next two years, he worked with Howard to ready his company for the conversion. Howard prepared information to meet the financial audit requirements of an IPO and encouraged David to get rid of all product lines that weren't environmentally friendly.

Lost Dreams

Howard wanted David to work closer with his executive team to improve upon their weaknesses. He thought David should try to retain them.

David had concerns about Howard's suggestion. He wasn't sure he had the right people *on the bus*. And even if he did, he didn't think they were all in the right seats.

Howard's retort was, "It cost time and money to recruit new people and your energy has to be on building, not replacing."

Two of the newest members, who had been with David for the past three years, had not fully bought into his vision. He couldn't quite identify his sense of unease, but he knew that some of it came from a conversation he had overheard. They were sitting by themselves in the lunch room when David walked in. He heard them talking about starting up another company. When he questioned them, they assured him they were quite happy where they were. David brought this to Howard's attention, but he didn't seem concerned. After a while, David let it go, thinking he was probably making an issue out of a non-existent problem.

Then it happened. First the operations executive quit. Next his sales leader left. David's hope of taking the company public slowly evaporated. His full attention was now placed on legal issues, and rebuilding leadership, sales, and confidence. He blamed Howard for this major oversight which weakened the company and would have repercussions for years to come. The gap that was left required David's full and immediate attention. Instead of concentrating on growth, David spent his days managing a very dysfunctional sales force and overseeing operations. He was seething with anger at Howard, who he thought should have been better prepared. He should have encouraged David to replace the two questionable executives. He also should have suggested hiring a temporary COO who could partner with David to get the company back to where it once was.

Like a caged animal, trapped and with no control over his destiny, David was frustrated and bitter.

Howard offered to stay on and help David get back on solid ground, but David refused. He had lost all trust in him. Howard was David's scapegoat. David fired Howard and never took the company public. It took four years to properly replace his leadership team. During that period, growth was stymied.

Eighteen years later, David still blames Howard for failure to take the company public. His bitterness and anger haven't subsided. In fact, it impedes his ability to lead and he contemplates selling the chain.

ACCOUNTABILITY

It is not only what we do, but also what we do not do, for which we are accountable.

Moliere

David blamed Howard for the fiasco. Instead of looking at himself, he pointed the finger outward. Had David stepped up to the plate, taken control of the situation, and replaced the two leaders in his own timeframe, this probably would not have happened. He would be running a public company today. But David refused to acknowledge his role in this, and so his agony was prolonged. He was left with unanswered questions, a lot of rage, and a privately held company that now showed shrinking profits. Even 18 years later, had David taken accountability for this event, he'd lighten up and have more access to some unanswered questions. He could also learn from mistakes made and move both himself and the company forward.

Failure to achieve a goal, no matter how small, can be an extremely powerful lesson, though quite difficult to let in. To take ownership, you must first claim that you made a mistake. Let me reiterate. You must claim to have made the mistake and not blame it on anyone else, no matter how wrong the other person was.

Taking ownership is often a humbling process, for you must push your ego aside. Ego wants to keep you safe, so will give you signals not to show any failure. It isn't that the greatest leaders haven't failed; they've failed more than the common person. They've learned how to push their egos aside and take responsibility, even publicly, for their failures. And they always take responsibility when others are involved because ultimately they are in charge of their company.

Great leaders have practiced accountability and know that by acknowledging their failures or mistakes comes freedom. It's a declaration to themselves and to others that they aren't perfect and are willing to take risks, fall down, accept the gift of failure, and move on. I say the gift of failure, because there is always a great gift, if not many, given to us when we fail. The gift is the lesson learned. Once you learn that lesson, chances are you'll never let that happen again. And if you do let it happen again, you'll be better prepared for the outcome and how to handle it.

Ownership

Being accountable is taking ownership—ownership of the desired outcome and the actual result. Whether the results you want to have happen do happen, or the results you want to have happen don't happen, when you own the outcome—you are being accountable. Ownership is realizing the breach between the desired outcome and the outcome you got.

When you take ownership of an outcome, you are telling the truth. You are acknowledging out loud what went wrong. You're also admitting your shortcomings. It takes courage to be ultimately responsible, especially when others are involved and witness what happened. Ego will step in and want you to *look good*. But when you take ownership, you will gain great freedom—there is nothing more to hide. This leads to more confidence and greater personal power.

Here is the added benefit that no one tells you about. As you take ownership, so will others. They'll have to. You've opened the door creating higher standards. With this comes more productivity because people will spend less time complaining and more time doing what they need to do.

YOUR WORD

He that is good for making excuses is seldom good for anything else.

Ben Franklin

Accountability and commitment go hand in hand. Commitment is the giving of your word to something. When you give your word, you are making a promise or pledge. You are saying, "I will do what I promised." This is very powerful. Your word gives you the opportunity to take control of your life, setting the direction and then following through, instead of living it by happenstance. When you live your life from following through on your word, there are no accidents. Miracles appear, as if to reward you for not falling short, even though at times you may not want to carry out what you promised. You become an active player on the field of your own life, not a passive spectator, watching and wishing things could be better. You have a say in your own life.

You may be shaking your head right now, saying no, this is not me. You may be thinking this is just so simple. Why wouldn't anyone follow through on what they say? But everyone at some time, even the best of us, falls short in this area.

In the early stages of coaching a business leader, they will typically tell me that this is not a problem area for them. But as we get deeper in to it, they realize that they've just skimmed the surface of what it really means to bring commitment to anything they do.

Commitment and Trust

Making a commitment and then keeping it builds trust. People like working with people they can count on. When they can count on you—you are *count-on-able*. And you can count on yourself. When you are count-on-able, nothing moves you from your promise, no matter what the obstacles are. You are not giving in to your emotions, such as "I don't feel like it," or "I don't have any time," or "why did I say that, I didn't really mean it." You create a boundary that will not be crossed. You declare that this is the way it shall be, nothing short of that will be acceptable. You hold on to this belief firmly.

People Remember

Your word precedes you, wherever you go. People remember when you keep your promises. They also remember when you don't. How do you want to be seen in the world? More importantly, how do you want to see yourself?

Breaking your commitments may bother others, but in the long run, it is you who will be most affected.

But what about those times when you absolutely can't keep your word? When you catch yourself wanting to get out of a commitment, break a promise, or go off and live it up instead of keeping your word, be aware of just that—you are breaking your word, crossing your own boundary. The difference is you are aware of it and now can take ownership for breaking your word. As strange as it may sound, this too is accountability. Yes, you broke your promise, but you owned it. And if you were really accountable, you let the other person know way ahead of time that you will be rescheduling—knowing that you won't cancel out with them again.

As you begin to diligently hold yourself to your commitments, you'll experience a life with fewer complications and less stress.

Blame

Accountability is the key to freedom. It puts you in the driver's seat and allows you control. When you blame someone else, you give up control. Blame will not reverse or solve a problem. It will, however, cause complications to a situation, creating resentment, guilt, and mistrust. It clouds clear thinking and moves you from getting at the root of a problem. Resist giving up ownership and you'll resist giving up your freedom.

Why Bother?

When people have a *why bother* attitude, it is a clear indication that accountability is missing. If you notice that people look bored, tired, dull, frustrated, or restrained at work, there is probably a *why bother* attitude in the atmosphere. You may hear this coming out of the mouths of employees:

"Why should I bother? Nothing ever changes here. I am powerless to do anything. Nobody ever listens anyway."

When you feel out of control and don't know what to do, check in with your accountability. I can guarantee you that somewhere accountability isn't present. Ask yourself: Am I doing what I said? If the answer is no, get back on track. Re-examine your commitment or promise. If change is to happen, it must begin with you.

Excuses versus Freedom

There are no excuses in accountability. Here is the hard cold fact: you either are accountable or you're not. There's no in between. Don't try to explain away what happened, as if you're not part of the reason for why it occurred. Acknowledge instead that you were a contributing factor. When you tell the impeccable truth about what occurred, you will uncover a new found freedom.

BEING ACCOUNTABLE

Accountability is not something you do. It's a way you are being. The statement *I am accountable* does not mean you're doing anything. It means you are *being* something.

Accountability is being the owner of the outcome, whether it's good or bad. Suppose I put a cup of coffee down on a table full of best selling books in a book store. Someone comes along and accidentally knocks over the cup drowning the books in hot coffee. Sure, the person who knocked over the coffee is accountable, but so am I. I put down a full cup of coffee in a place it didn't belong.

Exceptional leaders are pro-active about being accountable, they take an offensive position with it. They look for it, demand it from others, and know when it isn't present.

Once accountable, you can make changes to drive results, correct mistakes, or turnaround potential failure because you're back in the driver's seat. Ultimately no matter how hard you try, you can't control what someone else does or doesn't do—even though you'd like to. But there is one person you can control—and that is you. When David blamed Howard, it left him helpless and a victim of circumstance. There's definitely no control, no power, in that.

When you take ownership of something you did (wrong) or something you didn't complete, you are choosing not to be a victim. David became a victim by not choosing ownership.

Years later, David acknowledged that he should have taken a firm stand on replacing some of his leadership team. He realized the mistake was a fateful one. Had he replaced his team, or at least taken ownership for what happened, he could have possibly averted the disaster that lead to dismantling the hope of taking his company public and obstructing future growth. But by the time he realized this, he was worn down and ready to sell the company.

Don't underestimate the power of accountability or the lack of it. The smallest thing overlooked could turn into a disaster. It's like a trickle of water coming into your basement during a heavy rain. No matter how well you seal the wall, if you miss one tiny area, the water will find its way through and cause damage.

ASK YOURSELF

The following questions will help you to look at your accountability. Take some quality time to get quiet, close your eyes, and ask yourself these questions.

1. What have you promised to do, that you haven't done? Include calls and e-mails to return, conversations that need to be had, goals that haven't been met, etc.
2. What stops you from keeping your promise in those areas you listed?

(continued)

3. How do you feel when you break your word?
4. What do you need to let go of to become accountable?
5. What stops you from holding others accountable?
6. How much significance do you put on your word? If you were to tape record yourself for a week and replay your promises, would you have kept them all?
7. When you make a commitment, what is the impact it has on you and others when you don't keep it?

PRACTICE THIS

The following four practices will assist you in *being* accountable. Being accountable will produce a life without excuses and blame. You will be free from the internal chains of guilt, regret, and blame.

Practice #1: Keep Your Word

Make promises. Then deliver on them. Period. Yes, I know this is easier said than done. And I also know that it is almost impossible to always do what you promise. But if you got into the mindset that every time you were about to make a commitment, you stopped and thought about it for a moment before promising, you would be moved in the direction to keep your word more and more.

When you pause before you commit, ask yourself, *is this something that I want to commit to?* If it is, go ahead and make the commitment. And then carry through on it. No excuses accepted.

If you don't think you will be able to do it, then don't commit. And if you have some doubt, then think it through. Don't commit to anything unless you have every intention of following through.

It is much more powerful to not commit than to commit and not do what you promised. For as you do, you gain internal power. And as you default, you lose it.

As you become more conscious of the commitments you make, you'll build the muscle. You'll notice that people rely on you—they trust that what you say is gold.

Make at least one commitment a day and keep it for the next 21 days. It takes 21 days to create a practice that will begin to feel more natural and not as forced. To do this become vigilante that your words match your intentions. Don't tell someone you'll call them back, and then you don't. Even if you never see them again you want to avoid putting that type of energy out there. Put out what you want to come back to you.

Starting today, right now, promise to live up to your agreements. Live your life from keeping your word. It is a powerful place to come from.

Practice #2: Throw Your Cap Over the Wall

You've given your word and now you have to follow through on it. But when the time comes, you find there are many obstacles that block you from keeping it. That is the curious thing about keeping your word. Once you commit to something, obstacles pop up out of nowhere. There is only one thing to do when obstacles occur. Throw your cap over the wall.

U.S. President John F. Kennedy is a great example of this. He was determined to put a man on the moon, a feat that was unheard of in the early 1960s. In a speech, he told the following story:

> Frank O'Connor, the Irish writer, tells in one of his books how, as a boy, he and his friends would make their way across the countryside, and when they came to an orchard wall that seemed too high and too doubtful to try and too difficult to permit their voyage to continue, they took off their hats and tossed them over the wall—and then they had no choice but to follow them.[1]

Their caps became their promise. Now they'd have to follow through on it. In the wake of your commitments, when obstacles come up, throw your cap over the wall. Then go get it.

Practice #3: Construct an Arch, Then Stand Under It

Ancient Roman engineers had a remarkable tradition. When an arch was constructed and the last stone was hoisted into its place, the engineer assumed accountability for his work in the most profound way. He stood under the arch. If it was going to fall apart, he would be the person under it.

In everything that you do, your name is stamped on it. Be like the Roman engineers. Do it right. Make sure it is up to your standards. Several years ago I visited Rome and the ancient ruins. Do you know what I saw? After almost two thousand years, those arches are still standing.

Imagine a company full of accountable people. They promise something, fulfill on it, and it is done right. High standards are set.

Sure we all fall short at some time or another, but again, the point here is to build the muscle in order to drive for excellence. Accountability can change not only the performance of your business, but your life, and on a grander note—the world. Like the Roman arches, it may be the truest path to long-lasting success.

Practice # 4: Being Accountable

The great news about accountability is that as you practice it, so will others around you—they'll have no choice. Once you value this way of being, you'll hold others to it as well. However, until you become accountable, others won't either. The following is a step-by-step process to get you building the practice of being accountable—time after time after time.

1. When you create a goal or target, use specific measurable results and timeframes. It's not a goal if these are missing.
2. Let others know your goal, enroll them in supporting you.
3. Throw your cap over the wall. Diligently keep to your commitment, no matter what obstacles appear. Fight the desire to give up, give in, or divert your attention.
4. However, if you do divert, get back on track immediately. Don't wait until tomorrow. Recommit at once.
5. Evaluate the outcome. Did you make the goal? What worked? What didn't? Get honest with yourself. If you didn't attain the goal, uncover what happened. Did you fail to live up to your commitments? Toss out any blame, excuses, guilt, or justifications. Accept what is.
6. Once you have examined your role, acknowledge it out loud. Let people know you are taking responsibility for what happened. Be the example for others. Let them know they can count on you to acknowledge your wins and losses.
7. Ask others to do the same. Hold them accountable. Request that they set their defenses aside, step up to the plate, and take accountability for what happened. This will help them to grow and improve.
8. Use each mistake as a learning tool. Keep your mind and your heart open.
9. Okay, so now you're ready to set another goal. Remember, what you say, you must then do. Do not let time, money, too much work, or other excuses keep you from your commitment.

SUMMARY

☑ When you are accountable, you own the outcome, whether it's good or bad.
☑ Your word precedes you, don't give it lightly.
☑ Do what you promise.
☑ You can't hold others accountable, until you hold yourself accountable first.
☑ Accountability creates learning and growth. It is the key to freedom.
☑ Extraordinary leaders don't fall prey to being victims—they hold themselves accountable. Ordinary leaders use blame and excuses and are, therefore, victims of circumstance.
☑ The strongest leaders are on the offense, with hands-on commitment and follow through—being proactive about being accountable.
☑ Throw your cap over the wall. Then go get it.
☑ Do your best, then test it to make sure. Build your company like the Romans built arches.

NOTE

1. John F. Kennedy, Remarks at the Dedication of the Aerospace Medical Health Center, November 21, 1963.

9

Build the Business You've Imagined

> You are a child of the universe, no less than the moon and the stars; you have a right to be here. And whether or not it is clear to you, no doubt the universe is unfolding as it should.
>
> Max Ehrmann, "Desiderata"

A BUDDING ENTREPRENEUR AND THE TRICKSTER

Inevitably when you set a monumental goal, one that will make a big difference in your life if attained, the universe becomes a trickster—throwing you a curve ball. It taunts you by testing your determination and staying power, as if to see if you're really serious about getting what you say you want. This is exactly what happened to Lisa after she made the commitment to start up her own business.

One night she awoke in a pool of sweat. Six months ago she left a job in corporate America to follow her dreams of starting a business. The defining moment was upon her. She needed more clients. Although happy with her decision to get out of the rat race, this early stage entrepreneur was worried. She struggled to find new business and worried about going broke. After lunch one day with some friends, she reached in her wallet to split the bill and found only coins. Credit cards were of no use to her now—she had already maxed them out. Aware that she was facing a crossroad, she knew that if she didn't do something fast, she'd be back on the doorsteps of the corporate world.

A determined woman, Lisa knew in her heart that she was on the right path. That's what made this all so frustrating. She just had to figure out how to make it work. With questions came doubt and loss of confidence.

> Why in the world did I leave a secure corporate position to struggle like this?
> Do I really have what it takes to make this work?
> If I can't get to $100,000 this year, how am I ever going to get to my big goal of $10 million in 20 years?

The healthy part of Lisa would not hold on to those negative questions for long. She kept telling herself she was on the right path.

Burn the Ships

Lisa had worked at a Boston CPA firm for eight years before launching this company. Her father, a third-generation owner of a manufacturing organization, was preparing for retirement and encouraged Lisa to join him in his company instead of going out on her own. But Lisa had worked there summers and holidays and decided long ago that was not the environment she wanted. Her father knew that Lisa was stubborn and to argue with her would be senseless. So he gave her his blessings. He told Lisa that he trusted her decisions, and she should follow her own path.

Now six months later, she was in this current state of high anxiety. Sleep evaded her most nights. She would awake exhausted from tossing and turning. After one too many sleepless nights, she met her father for lunch. She told him she was up against a wall and didn't know what to do. Any savings that she had was running out and soon she wouldn't be able to pay the rent where she lived.

Her father listened carefully, while hiding his concern and replied, "I know you will find a way to make this work out. Don't give up. Burn all ships. You can do this."

The saying *burn all ships* came from a legendary event that happened in 1519. Hernán Cortés, the Spanish conquistador set out to the Yucatan Peninsula with a small group of 500 soldiers and 11 ships to conquer the Aztecs and capture their treasures. He knew that his men would be at a disadvantage because they didn't know this foreign land and the Aztecs had a large empire that was over six centuries old. The task of winning was huge. The night before the battle, Cortés sent some of the men back to their 11 ships and ordered them to be burned. Next morning as the men awoke and saw the ships on fire, Cortés said, "If we are going home, we are going home in their ships." If they were going to win and get back home, Cortés had to take away the option of failure. They either had to win or die. Upon winning, they took the riches and went home aboard the Aztec's ships.[1]

Lisa got the message. She understood what real determination was and she wouldn't give up. She would be like Cortés and back herself up against the wall, with no way out, only through. Her father was a wise man. He knew this was the first of many difficult times she'd face as a business owner. His encouragement was needed and felt. He didn't tell her what to do or how to do it, he just believed in her and let her know that. Many times that kind of support is just what we need to jump through our own hurdles.

That night, feeling less burdened after her talk with her dad, she put together a plan to attract more clients to her young CPA firm. Lisa would do whatever she needed to do to make this work—*no*—to make this damn successful, she thought! She was going to build the business of her dreams.

FIVE STEPS

Lisa read everything she could get her hands on about business development. When she was introduced to me, her desire to grow her business and to become successful was palpable. The major roadblock for Lisa was her self-belief. She lacked that gutsy consistent conviction to succeed. It would be a difficult journey if she didn't go to work on this area. But she was determined. Her father's voice rang loud in her head and she refused to let him down.

Having more clients meant her business would grow which would lead to Lisa's dream of financial freedom. As we worked together, Lisa learned five crucial steps to do just that.

Step #1 Visualize, Then Write It Down

The first step in her action plan was to visualize, then write down her goals. I asked her to do this many times during the day. Then she would take one major goal and focus on that for 21 days or until it was achieved. This would help her not to diffuse energy from that one goal.

According to the Silva Life System, "Visualize what you want and write it down fifteen times in a row, once a day, until you obtain it."[2]

According to authors Jack Canfield, Dr. Wayne Dyer, and many others who wrote testimonials on the Silva Life System website,[3] it has helped them overcome illness, become more intuitive, get what they wanted—more money, write a book, etc.

Lisa began her visualization by asking a question. Questions will help you get clear on the goal.

She asked herself, "What is the size of the business I want, and when do I want to achieve it?"

She said she wanted a $10 million business in 20 years. That was a very long-term goal. I told her of Parkinson's Law: work expands so as to fill the time available for its completion. If a goal is set to be reached in seven months, it will take seven months. If the same goal is set to take three months, that is how long it will take. I suggested that she shorten her timeframe of 20 years. She did. Lisa made the goal 10 years and was pleased with that. She said it became more real for her. It was do-able. Things were beginning to heat up.

Step #2 Draw the Picture in Your Mind

The next step was to picture the entire business as it would be in 10 years. Where would it be located? How many offices would she have? What was her niche market? Would the offices be in other countries? How many employees? What was the typical profile of her employees: age, sex, personality, work ethics, family, salary, and experience? What would her office look like: colors, furniture, pictures, windows, and her desk? Lisa had to visualize everything. Not one thing could be overlooked.

She then wrote it all down. One time was enough.

Step # 3 Feel It, Believe It

Your mind doesn't know the difference between what is real and what is imaginary. This is the *nail the coffin shut* step to building the business you want. Lisa had to feel what it would be like to own a $10 million business. She did some more writing, examining how she thought she'd feel when she reached her goal. This step is critical because when she felt it, her mind wouldn't know the difference between whether she really achieved it or not.

Frank Lloyd Wright said, "The thing always happens that you really believe in; and the belief in a thing makes it happen."

Lisa was shaping her mind to think that her goal had already been met.

Step #4 Read It

Now that she completed the first three steps, she was ready for the fourth. Minimally, each night before retiring and every morning upon rising, she was to read what she had written about her visualization of the business and the feelings it would bring her. After reading it, she was to sit for a few moments. Close her eyes and envision it. Let it sink in.

Step # 5 Develop an Action Plan

As Lisa completed these steps, a shift occurred. She felt more at peace. She was able to speak with more conviction to prospects. She got clear on the value of her services.

She put together an action plan taking her through all of the steps to building a $10 million business and the dates she'd achieved them. This took some time, but it was well worth it. Since her mindset and confidence had shifted, she was ready to execute her plan. Had she tried to develop and implement a plan from her old mindset, she would have failed.

The following is an example of Lisa's Action Plan (© Leadership & Executive Development, LLC).

The Appendix B has a blank action plan that you can use.

1. Write your goal in simple format.
A goal has three elements: What you want, by when, and how you'll know you got there:
Lisa: I want to have $10 million in revenue by December 31, 2019.

2. In order of priority, list the three *greatest* challenges you are currently facing around that goal.
Lisa:
A. Not enough time.
B. Not enough resources.
C. Not knowing how to find and hire the right people.

3. List two areas of personal self-growth that will support reaching your goal.

Lisa:

A. Sales training.

B. Strengthen my listening.

4. Considering you had all the resources and support, what is the *number one greatest change* you would like to make to your:

Give a separate answer for each.

A. Life as a whole: Lisa: *feel less stress*

B. Physical self, your health and well being:
   Lisa: *make regular health check-ups and keep them.*

C. Intellectual, mental self

D. Emotional, spiritual self

E. Work life

F. Family life

G. Social relationships outside of work

H. Relationship with time

I. Relationship with money

J. Relationship with yourself

K. Leadership team (if applicable)

L. Partners (if applicable)

M. Peers

N. Employees or vendors

O. Company

6. As best as you can, describe where you will be/want to be with your goal, in:

Lisa:

A. One year: Put away $50,000 after taxes.

B. Two years: Business bringing in $1 million in revenue.

C. Three years: Business revenue is $3 million.

D. Five years: Business revenue is $5 million.

7. For each year above in question #6, write a short plan with five steps to make it happen. *I don't know* is not an answer.

Lisa:

A. One year:

   1. Take a sales training course.
   2. Hire an executive coach.
   3. Hire a great financial advisor.
   4. Find the right assessment tools for hiring the right people.
   5. Develop a marketing plan.

B. Two years:

C. Three years:

D. Five years:

ASK YOURSELF

Now it's your turn. If you're reading this book, it's because you want to have a better business. You want to finally build the business you've always imagined. So let's get started. Take some quality time to get quiet, close your eyes, and ask yourself these questions.

1. What would you attempt to do if you knew you couldn't fail?
2. What is your goal? By when do you want to reach it?
3. What is in the way to achieve it? Notice your mindset.
4. What would you have to let go of to shift your mindset?
5. Are you willing to *burn the ships* to get what you want?

PRACTICE THIS

Let's put this into practice. The following six practices will help you to remove all obstacles. Read these daily to keep yourself on track. Don't think you can skip even one day. One day turns into another day and before you know it, you'll have forgotten how to take the steps to build the business of your dreams.

Practice #1: Set the Goal, Then Strap Yourself In

Clarity is essential here. It is time to get very clear about your goal. What do you want? Try not to pay as much attention right now to how you'll get it yet. At this point, all you need to do is to get crystal clear on *what* it is. Once you have it, write it down and post it in several locations. The more times you can read it during the day, the better. I post mine next to my computer on my desk in my office, on my nightstand by my bed, and on my mirror. I absolutely can't miss them there. Visualize the goal. See yourself reaching it. How does it feel? This is an important part of the process. When your brain connects with how it feels it doesn't differentiate if it is real or not. And you're making your goal a reality. Feeling it is like it's already happening.

1. Set your goal.
2. Write it down.
3. Visualize having it.
4. Imagine how it will feel.
5. Read it twice daily.

Now strap yourself in for a wonderful ride of rewards!

Practice #2: Believe

Believe that you can have the business you desire. Kill off any thoughts that are not moving you in a positive direction. These thoughts may sound like: *I don't know how to build a $10 million business. Who am I to do this? I don't have time to follow my plan every day. Will I lose my friends when I become rich?*

These thoughts are destructive. Get rid of them before they take hold. When I have a destructive thought pop into my head I say, *thank you for that thought. I know you are trying to protect me, but I don't need you right now. Good bye.*

Practice #3: Watch for Signs

This is the fun part. You've done a large part of the work. You've created your goal, visualized it, can feel what it will be like when you achieve it, and put together a plan to get there. Now watch for the fun signs to show up that you're on the right track. Lisa told me that sometimes the signs flooded her. This made her laugh. She'd start to find money on the ground over and over again—this is a sign. Phones begin ringing off the hook. Suddenly referrals and new business come in from nowhere. A deal you've been working on may unexpectedly close. Everything is flowing.

Signs let you know that everything is working in the perfect order to get you what you want. I know this may sound like woo-woo stuff. But don't disregard it. Many people who accumulated large masses of wealth have set these practices into motion and realize that signs are examples of the alignment of your goals with your heart's desire—a perfect match that brings great rewards.

Practice #4: Find a Mentor or Coach

Find someone who believes in you and will stand for what you want to achieve, even when you can't. All great coaches have coaches and mentors. I've also had one. It's a limiting mindset if you think you can do it all yourself. Another viewpoint gives you a more expansive prospective. Sometimes we're just too close to the issues to make much sense of them. Be sure to find someone you have to pay. The reason I say that is when you pay someone, you put skin in the game. The more you pay them, the more you're likely to *burn all ships* and not leave an option for failure. Find the best coach you can. The return on investment will be beyond your wildest imagination. The best athletes and superstars all have coaches—the best ones they can find.

Practice #5: Come Back to Your Intention

When Lisa would slip back into the fear of not having enough clients or money, she brought her attention back to her intention. Why was she doing what she was doing? She wanted to help other business owners grow their businesses and their profits. Secondly, she didn't want to let her father down. She wanted to show him how right he was to believe in her.

Put something at stake. For me it is this. If I don't get to do full out what I love to do—which is coaching business leaders to become successful and live a life of meaning—then I will not have fulfilled my own purpose while I'm living here on earth.

Set up your intention. Then GO FOR IT! *Burn the ships*!

Practice #6: Be Open to Possibilities

Realize that you cannot control everything. In fact, if we think about it, we really can't control much—no one can. Yet we're comforted by the thoughts that we can control a lot. When we let go of control, we open the door to hidden possibilities such as more money coming in when we least expect it. When you're feeling stressed, ask yourself, what am I trying so hard to control? Then let go of it, even for just one day. Look to see if you really need to control it anymore. Is the stress worth it? Give up your hold on how you think things will turn out. It's much more fun to have things come to you freely and easily. Let Go!

SUMMARY

- ☑ Get crystal clear on your goal for your business. Include the date you want to achieve it by. Write it down.
- ☑ Visualize your goal.
- ☑ Feel how it will be when you achieve the goal.
- ☑ Read your goal at least twice a day, preferably in the morning and before bedtime.
- ☑ Create an action plan to reach your goal. What do you need to do to get there?
- ☑ Believe that you can make this happen.
- ☑ Gently let go of any destructive thoughts.
- ☑ Watch for fun signs to show you are on the right path.
- ☑ Don't do it alone. Find a mentor or coach to support you in achieving your goal.
- ☑ Put something at stake for you to reach your goal. What are you really doing this for? What is your intention?
- ☑ Open yourself to possibilities and they will begin to fly in.
- ☑ Let go!

NOTES

1. Lee Kemp, "Success Secrets from 3: Message #15—'Burn the Ships,' " Kemps Korner—Live, September 22, 2007, http://successsecretsatkempskorner .blogspot.com/2007/09/burn-ships.html.

2. "Silva Life System Online Course," Silva Life System and MindValley LC, 2009, http://www.silvalifesystem.com/online/lessons/1-intro.

3. Silva Life System, http://www.silvalifesystem.com.

10

Remember—The Coolest Wealth Is Your Health

To keep the body in good health is a duty ... otherwise we shall not be able to keep our mind strong and clear.

Buddha

PUTTING OTHERS FIRST

When the stock market tanked in 2008, Anne felt the ramifications. It had been eight years ago that she had started up her recruitment business. Although recruiters were still needed to find employees, companies were drastically cutting back as unemployment rose. Anne's business took a nose-dive. She was under constant pressure to increase sales in a job market that was all but dead.

Described as someone who likes to help others, Anne always had a smile on her face, and was the type of person that people gathered around at parties. Her attitude was positive and contagious. However, the price she paid for putting others' needs before her own was high—the highest price one could pay.

As the economy tumbled and Anne's business demanded more of her attention, her stamina decreased. She spent additional hours at the office, replacing meals with coffee. She became addicted to the sugary caffeinated cappuccinos from the automatic machines in the nearby convenience store. She arrived late to meetings, trying hard to squeeze in all that she could before she got there—and often showed up frazzled.

As a 40-something, single mom, she prided herself on being home for dinner most nights with her three children. And although her heart was in the right place, it was countered by the additional pressure she put on herself. Her family still complained that she didn't spend enough time with them. Everyone seemed to want something from her.

The Offer

Years before, Anne had declined an offer from an international company that was interested in buying her firm. She was a young and unproven business woman at the time, yet had built a company worthy of their exploration. Within five years, she had created a company with multi-offices and seven figures in revenue. The interested party presented her with an offer that was undervalued. She knew she could get more, but she wasn't ready to sell. The business was just hitting its stride. But today with so much stress, she regretted not taking them up on their offer.

THE PRICE PAID

Anne's business model had worked well up to this point. Before the current state of economy went into its tailspin, she was on target to increase revenues almost 30 percent from the prior year. Her business model was strong. She had great advisors and a dedicated team. As growth continued at a healthy clip, she hired a business developer. He became a valued employee and would have had the opportunity to turn her company into a huge success had the financial world not crashed.

Anne cared about her employees as much as she did her clients. This was good news for all—for people pleasers like to make everybody happy. But their happiness came at a cost to Anne. The one person Anne needed to take care of the most was often neglected—this person was Anne, who put herself last.

A Trip to the Doctor

Although you'd never know it because she was always smiling, Anne felt lousy. She was concerned for her business. Any balance she had in life was long gone the day she started up the company. Anne was no different from most entrepreneurs. She knew stress intimately. It was a familiar bed partner. When times were tense, her stomach would chime in by feeling achy. She often wondered if she was developing an ulcer. Each time she felt pain, she promised to cut out caffeine, but never did.

Many entrepreneurs tell me that running a company takes a toll on their physical and mental health. They report that it has contributed to weight change, lack of sleep, decreased energy, depression, and irritability.

Three months after Anne's business continued to lose profit and began to take a loss, she landed in the doctor's office with a diagnosed stress-related condition. She had a new developed symptom—migraine headaches. This was one condition that stopped her from working. She couldn't think, read, or listen to anyone when she had a migraine. The only thing she could do was take to bed when these episodes occurred.

The doctor had known Anne since she was in her twenties. She hadn't been in for a physical in years and he couldn't believe how much she had changed. She looked 10 years older than her chronological age. Her weight gain was almost 20 pounds since he last saw her. For a short woman, the pounds could not be hidden. Her hair had lost its shine and her teeth had yellowed from smoking. Anne was on sleeping medication and still tossed and turned all night. She admitted that at times she took a sedative during the day to calm her mind and nerves. She was concerned that she would become addicted to the medication, but couldn't stop. All she did was work, she complained to her physician. She had little time for much else.

Going to the doctor's office was not easy. Anne had been avoiding it as long as she could. But as her symptoms worsened, she bit the bullet and dragged herself there. Together they reviewed her exercise regime and diet. Quite simply, there was no exercise happening, stated Anne. An athlete in school, she now had to relinquish keeping fit to putting in more time at the office. Her doctor grimaced as she told him how she ate. For breakfast she grabbed a muffin with two cups of coffee. Her lunch was typically fast food—anything that could be eaten on the go. Dinners weren't different. On her way home from work, she'd stop at a fast food chain to pick up the evening meal for her family. Sometimes they didn't eat until eight o'clock. She never took supplements because they upset her stomach even more. Anne complained that she was just a mess and felt like she was falling apart.

The doctor did some testing and told her he'd call with the results in a couple of days. Meanwhile, he directed her to lose 20 pounds, stop smoking, cut out caffeine, and immediately discontinue any sedatives. He also said to start to exercise and eat healthier meals. Right, thought Anne, like she had time to do any of this.

L'CHAIM—TO LIFE!

Don't Turn Away from This Message

If you're reading this, you may be cringing. You may see parts of yourself in Anne. You may even feel the urge to skip this chapter. But don't. I know this topic is difficult for many. Most of us struggle with weight, eating nutritiously, exercise, or getting enough rest. Many entrepreneurs tell me—it's all part of the job. Ignoring your health does not have to be part of the job. Being in any physical or mental pain does not have to be part of the job. No job should create that. Our bodies cannot sustain that type of injurious activity over time. Like Anne, if not handled immediately, it can turn into chronic illness and disability. So don't turn away.

Good News, Bad News

Two days later the doctor called and said he had good news. None of the blood work showed signs of diabetes or other disease. Her cholesterol, however, was high. He told Anne she was lucky. She had habits of an unhealthy person. She had gotten to him in time and they could begin to make change. Anne wanted to take care of herself. She had to. She celebrated with a bag of cookies. Two weeks later, she was out of commission for ten days with the flu. On the ninth day, I got a call from Anne.

CLEANSING

Anne explained her situation. She started with the history of her business and what wasn't working. Then she outlined her poor health habits. When she was done, she cried. I knew what Anne couldn't realize just yet. These were cleansing tears. She was about to embark on a new journey, one that incorporated good health habits. Here is the great news: when Anne got healthy, her business was sure to follow.

The Fear Factor

Anne suffered from fear. Who hasn't faced fear in their lives, especially if you're a business owner? Managing fear when facing risk, as you embark on a new path, is what successful people have come to know and accept. Anne had not learned how to manage her fears. Instead she turned to caffeine, food, or medication to help her through.

As I worked with Anne, she began to understand that when she was fearful, she risked making poor decisions or no decisions at all. That lead to stagnation or analysis paralysis. Analysis paralysis comes from over analyzing something so much that you tend not to do anything for fear of making a mistake.

Trust

We all have experienced coming to a crossroad and not knowing which way to go. Sometimes we have good information to make our decision and then hope it is the right one. Other times our information is limited or non-existent and we have to take a leap in faith as we decide on our course. Having faith that things will turn out no matter what choice we make is truly a leap of faith. We do this every day as we decide to hire someone, take on a new client, invest in a stock—all of these are leaps of faith. We don't know the outcome at the moment, we're trusting that it will work out. Having faith is trusting in yourself and trusting in the universe to provide you with what you need when you need it. When you can come from trust, you are at peace. When you come from doubt and worry, you aren't. This causes a desire to soothe the doubt and worry with some temporary comfort, but long-range harm, such as smoking, drinking, or overeating.

There was a great lesson for Anne to learn if she was ready. She was.-
Counter-Play

Anne based all of her decisions on playing it safe. This was not how she had started her business, because she had to take a risk to leave her job and start up this company. But over time with rejection from the outside world, loss of revenue, and poor decision making based on fear, inevitably it would bring her to this exact place. Her indecisiveness came from fear of loss. Anne had created a mentality of scarcity versus a mentality of abundance. She held on to everything she had as if she could lose it instead of viewing it from the perspective that there is plenty more out there, enough for everyone—including her.

Anne was looking at all her choices through the lens of fear. Fear took her off focus. Without focus she went from one task to another and never completed anything, worrying about everything. Although she had adapted this operating style, she knew it was not one to lead to a successful outcome. And eventually it would erode her health.

Before Anne could conquer fear and begin to make sound decisions, she would have to gain better balance in her life and health. She needed to take care of herself by getting enough rest, exercising and stretching, eating healthy meals, taking supplements, and doing mind-clearing exercises such as meditation, yoga, tai chi, or qigong. Yet many entrepreneurs like Anne say they have *no time* for such a daily regime. But the costs of stress can be crippling. Without good health, a leader has limited capacity to think clearly, make sound decisions, and lead with spirit. After all, if physical or mental capability are at risk, the consequences can be burn out or long-term disability.

ENTREPRENEURIAL FITNESS QUIZ

That night I asked Anne to complete the Entrepreneurial Fitness Quiz. This assessment is designed to gain clarity on areas that aren't aligned with your well-being. Think of it as a physical, mental, and spiritual fitness balancing in order to bring you more vitality. You'll also have an opportunity to take this quiz at the end of this chapter in the *Practice This* section and in the Appendix A.

Results

At our next meeting, Anne and I reviewed the responses to the Entrepreneurial Fitness Quiz. It was clear that she was in great imbalance. We set up an action plan for her to immediately work on all areas that had low ratings and to bring them up.

Sometimes it takes someone else to say, *stop*, what are you doing to yourself? Do you want to continue to do this? Are you ready to feel better? Do you want to have a more positive impact on your company? If so, here is an action plan to get you there. I know that I've been in situations where I just wanted someone to help me stop doing a certain behavior and help me to set up a plan to move forward. Sometimes that's all we need to get us out of the muck. It seemed for Anne that was exactly what she needed. She took the plan and ran with it. We'll take a further look at how to build your plan in the practice strategies at the end of this chapter.

Anne saw how balance is ultimately the lifeline to an entrepreneur's long-term relationship with her business. Myopically driven by results, most entrepreneurs ignore the signs of physical and emotional distress and imbalance until one day, like Anne, they get a wake-up call. They end up at the doctor's office or in the emergency room. But work and play can be combined in a beautiful balance that will relieve and eliminate anxiety and tension and create a way to healthier habits. When Anne, for instance, could distinguish the sure signs of exhaustion, frustration, or anger, she used deep breathing and centering techniques and also included power napping. She would take 10 minutes to lie on her sofa in her office and cat nap. Waking refreshed, her mind was clear to make difficult decisions she faced daily. In the past she would reach for a cup of sugary caffeine. That would give her a great jolt of energy that was short-lasting. She would find herself with less energy and more exhaustion shortly after the jolt from the cup of java. Then she would grab another cup to get her next boost.

Anne changed how she managed her schedule so that she wasn't always running late. For instance, if she had to attend a meeting more than a six-hour plane flight away, she made it a policy to arrive one day ahead of schedule. She could get to her hotel room, relax and prepare for the next day. Waking up the next morning, she felt ready to conquer with more energy than ever before.

ASK YOURSELF

Congratulations! You've gotten to this point in the chapter. You hung in there. This means you're probably considering an alternative operating style to incorporate more well-being into your life. This is great news. As your well-being improves, so will the lifeline of your business.

Take some quality time to get quiet, close your eyes, and ask yourself these questions.

1. How many cups of caffeine or sugary drinks do you consume a day?
2. Do you drink alcohol every day? If so, be brutally honest and say how many glasses you have? If this doesn't apply, then how many drinks do you have a week?
3. Do you do illicit drugs or take prescription medications to help you stay calm, or less stressed during the day or evening?
4. How would it feel to know that you were in great health? What could you do that you can't do now?
5. What would your body look like if you exercised daily? How would that feel?
6. How would it feel to work from a place of centeredness—where you could automatically bring yourself to this place time and time again, no matter what?

PRACTICE THIS

Have you been thinking about making changes in your health habits, but just don't know how, or don't have the time? These practices will help you get organized to gain more energy, more balance, and more healthful living in the shortest period of time.

Although I personally use these practices daily and have benefited greatly from incorporating them into my life, each person's outcome will be different. A lot depends on where you are starting from with your current habits. I must insert a disclaimer here. There are no guarantees that this will work for you or that you'll achieve results indicated or any other results. Each person is different and much has to do with your physical and mental condition upon embarking on this course. I am not a medical doctor or psychologist and I'm not qualified to provide you with that type of information. Please check with your medical advisor or psychologist before starting any of these practices.

There are six practices described in this section which can help detect energy zappers, increase stamina, lessen stress, and gain a deeper connection to inner harmony. As you gain more balance in your life, you will find it to be the beacon to lighting the way to health and happiness. As you become more centered, energized, and happier, your business will become healthier too.

Practice #1: Take the Entrepreneurial Fitness Quiz

Directions:

    a. Rate each item 1–10; 10 being the most satisfied.
    b. If not a 10, explain what is missing for it not to be at a 10.
    c. List actions needed to get you to a 10.
    d. Commit to a date that the actions will be completed.

Let's use #1 as an example, with Anne's answers.

Example (Anne)

> 1. Physical Exam (annual check up, blood work, etc.)
>   A. Rating: 3
>   B. What's missing? I haven't been to see a doctor in over five years.
>   C. Actions: Make appointment. Get exam. Get blood work. Talk about stomach pains and migraines.
>   D. Date to be completed: October 31

1. Physical exam (annual checkup, blood work, etc.)
2. Eye exam
3. Dental exam
4. Mammogram (where applicable)
5. Gynecological or prostate exam (where applicable)
6. Colonoscopy (where applicable)
7. Nutrition and diet
8. Sleep (well-rested)

9. Exercise and physical activity
10. Mind-clearing exercises and relaxation, such as meditation, yoga, tai chi, or qigong
11. Addiction-free, such as: food, alcohol, drugs, tobacco, shopping, gambling, sex, work, etc.
12. Your house/home environment
13. Your office(s)
14. Your car
15. Your dress and grooming—inclusive of your clothes, shoes, jewelry, make-up, hair, nails, briefcase, handbags, glasses, etc.
16. Outstanding bills (personal) and accounts payable (business)
17. Unresolved legal matters
18. Financial debt
19. Your credit rating
20. Tax and financial records organized
21. Bank accounts reconciled
22. Income taxes prepared/filed
23. Investments (retirement, college, wealth-building, etc.)
24. Outstanding gifts and cards
25. Phone calls (to be returned)
26. E-mails (to be answered)
27. Borrowed items (to be returned)
28. Items borrowed by others (to be returned to you)
29. Up-to-date agreements made with others
30. Unresolved employee conversations/issues
31. Unresolved client/customer conversations/issues
32. Unresolved vendor conversations/issues
33. Unresolved professional advisor (accountant, lawyer, board member, consultant, or coach, etc.) conversations/issues
34. Spiritual well-being
35. Energy balance
36. Anything else

Practice #2: Begin at the End

After completing the Entrepreneurial Fitness Quiz, circle all items that you've rated seven or lower. Next choose three of those items and put a star after each one. For each starred item imagine you've taken the necessary actions to raise the rating to a 10. Even though it hasn't happened yet, imagine it has. How does that feel? Are you free of worry, guilt, or anxiety? Do you feel healthier or reassured?

Now you're ready to go for it. Take those three items and implement the actions you've listed. Give yourself a short time period to complete them. Perhaps it is just two days. Although you may not be able to visit the doctor for your annual check-up in two days, you've taken the action to make the appointment. After you've completed those three starred items, do the same thing again with three more items. Continue through your list at a quick pace.

Perhaps you can set an overall goal to complete the actions on your entire list within two weeks.

Don't forget, when you've completed going through your list to congratulate yourself for taking care of YOU!

Practice #3: Remember to Pause

Your morning may begin by rushing out of bed to get ready for the day. You get dressed, and may grab something to eat. Then you rush out of your home to get to your office. Once there, it is hectic. Things fly at you constantly and before you know it, it's time to go home. On your way home, you think about tomorrow and what you have to get done that didn't get done today. At home, your kids want your attention, but you're too busy working out *important* things, like how to fire an employee or tell someone that they're not doing a good job. You feel guilty that you haven't given your children quality time with you. In bed that night with all those thoughts, you have a restless sleep, until it's time to get up and do it all over again.

Here is a healthier alternative. During your day—pause. What I mean by pausing is this—do nothing, nothing at all. You may just want to sit in your chair and close your eyes and breathe deeply for a moment. Or you could get up and do a yoga stretch, breathing into that stretch as you hold it for a minute or two. Whatever you choose to do, do it slowly as you concentrate on your breathing. You will breathe life back into your body. Pausing between activities, appointments, conversations, or even before entering the office or your home will provide you with more clarity, calmness, presence, and even better sleep. It will help you to stop worrying about things that haven't happened or things that already took place. So pause every moment you can, and breathe. Make a game of it. Start now. Close your eyes and take five deep breaths. Do this many times throughout your day—every day!

Practice #4: Retrain Yourself

Create the image of a healthy, balanced business person. To actually become that person, you'll need some retraining. Here's how to begin. When you go for that extra jumbo muffin made from white flour and white sugar—think. At first that may be all you'll need to do. Think of that healthy person you imaged. Then if you still want to reach for that muffin, go ahead. But eat only half now. Save the other half for later. Or better yet, leave it for someone else to eat. If I'm going to eat something that isn't congruent with the way I see myself being and yet I still can't resist the temptation, then I'll take a *taste*. That way it doesn't control me. A taste is one or two bites. But that's it. Any more, is no longer a taste, it's a portion. This helps because then I'm not consumed by that muffin sitting on the kitchen counter just waiting for me. After I take the taste, I can move on.

Another way to retrain yourself is with exercise. Do some sort of physical activity or exercise daily. Build up the habit. If you don't feel like it one day, don't skip it entirely. Hold that place with some sort of lighter exercise or activity. Perhaps instead of walking 45 minutes, you take your dog for two 20 minute walks. Keep the exercise routine going, even when you don't want to. Find ways to retrain your thinking from the old you to the new you.

Practice #5: If Nothing Else, Then Dance

Dancing is a great exercise, a great way to release the happy hormones, endorphins, and is an alternative to drinking another cup of coffee, a cocktail, or eating something not good for you. I love to dance, although probably not great at it. But I don't really care how I look, it's how I feel that matters. If dancing isn't it for you, use it as a metaphor. What gets you going? Is it singing, playing the piano, painting, or photography? Find the path that leads to releasing those endorphins. Watch as the door to more joy opens.

Practice #6: Make Fitness the Key to Your Kingdom

When I was 15, my grandmother declared to me in front of my mother that I was getting fat. I was wearing this wool dress that wasn't flattering and it easily showed that I was gaining weight. My mother was furious with her. But I never felt hurt. I knew she was telling me the truth, although she probably could have done it more subtly—though it may not have had the impact on me that it did. I began an exercise regime that lasted through my teenage years, three pregnancies, building businesses, and up to today. My routine went from doing aerobics with Jane Fonda tapes to joining a gym, swimming during pregnancies, running, walking, hiking, weight training, yoga, and Pilates.

Do I love to exercise? Perhaps some days I do. But what I love is how I feel afterwards. I work out every morning. I rarely take a break from exercise. It would be like not brushing my teeth for a day. Over the years, it has just become a habit. I know that exercise and eating well has been the key to health, staying young inside and out, and feeling happy.

Start with an exercise that you like. Perhaps it's just walking. Begin with a mild walk. I listen to my mp3 with upbeat songs or a motivational presentation that I've downloaded. That way I combine physical exercise with some spirit lifting exercise at the same time. Add to your routine each week. Walk faster or put in more time. Before long, you'll be a no excuses entrepreneur for health.

I eat three meals a day. I eat a great big bowl of shredded wheat, oatmeal, or cream of wheat (not the instant kind) for breakfast. I throw in a handful of blueberries, ground flax seed, and walnuts. Then I pour in some vanilla flavored soy milk. For lunch, I'm usually on the run, and if I'm not eating a salad, I'll munch on a protein bar and have some fruit and a handful of nuts later in the day. For dinner it is well balanced with protein, green vegetables, and usually some starch. After dinner I'll take a chunk of dark chocolate or splurge on a handful of Good & Plenty (I allow this splurge into my diet). The key is to eat balanced meals, stop going on fad diets, and if you have to splurge, do so with just a taste. Make staying fit, healthy, and centered a way of being, not something you have to do. If I can do it, so can you! You'll begin to see results immediately.

SUMMARY

- ☑ A balance of work, play, fitness, nutrition, spirituality, and meditation is the best prescription for health and happiness.
- ☑ Be sure to pause in-between activities, and breathe.
- ☑ Eat three well-balanced meals and splurge with only a taste.
- ☑ Do some type of exercise daily—hold that place in your day for exercise.
- ☑ Retrain yourself. If you don't feel like exercising, do a lighter workout that day, but do something.
- ☑ Retrain your eating. When you want to reach for something unhealthy—think. Do you really want it? If yes, take a taste, not a portion.
- ☑ Get up to date on your medical care. Make doctors' appointments.
- ☑ Stress leads to low levels of energy. Fight stress with meditation, yoga, tai chi, or qigong.
- ☑ Find your own dance to release endorphins, the happy hormones.
- ☑ Envision the new you: healthy, balanced, spiritually alive, and relaxed. If you can see it, you can have it.

11

Walk between the Raindrops, but Stomp in the Puddles

The gem cannot be polished without friction, nor man perfected without trials.

Chinese proverb

DROWNING IN PUDDLES

Every entrepreneur starts their company with the hopes of great success. I've never met one who was excited to embrace difficult times. In fact most people want to run from them. Yet these difficult challenges help us to grow not only ourselves, but our companies. No doubt they can stop us dead in our tracks, leaving us no choice but to push our goals in the background and get in the current moment of the latest breakdown. But they also open our eyes to see things we missed and to learn things we need to become better skilled at. Difficult times open our hearts.

Tough challenges may be one of the most important factors in our self-development as business owners (and as human beings). It may be the key element for the type of success each entrepreneur dreams about. The very thing that we wish away may be just the thing we must embrace. And so it was with Eve.

Cleaning Out the Old

Eve, a petite woman who looked 10 years younger than her true age, came from a close-knit Italian family. Her mother's brother was her mentor and role model. Uncle Joe encouraged her to utilize all of her natural talents to become so successful she'd never have to rely on a man for income. But it was Mrs. Patrickson who stimulated her initial career thoughts.

In fourth grade, Eve knew what she wanted to be—a teacher as kind and caring as Mrs. Patrickson—a teacher who helped this shy girl to feel good about herself. Eve's path was set. After graduating from college with a degree in education, she worked in the inner city public school system that was ill-matched with her idealistic view of how children should be taught.

Her dreams faded moment by moment as guards escorted her each day to the car. She dared not stay long after the final bell because the school was situated between the turfs of two gangs where gunshots rang out often. Perhaps she could have lived through the gang wars, but it was her inability to change an antiquated system that led her to quit four years later.

As a single mother, her precious and precocious three old son, Jake, was the light of her life. He became the motivation she needed to overcome the crumbling images of a brilliant teaching career and to begin a job search. She entered the world of business and took various sales jobs—learning how to cold call and negotiate. Her source of income was commission driven. If she didn't close sales, she didn't eat. It was survival.

Opened for Business

With each company that employed Eve, she would reach the top of the commission scale and then inevitably they would decide she was earning too much money and cut her commissions. After a while this grew old. Uncle Joe's advice was, "step out on your own." He knew she was ready and told her he'd help finance the venture she chose. Still Eve did nothing.

One day when she had grumbled one too many times, Uncle Joe said, "Well, it's time Eve. You have no other course but to do something on your own."

This time Uncle Joe's message got through. The two things she knew how to do well were to sell and teach, so she began by teaching people in companies how to sell. Slowly more companies became her clients.

As for running a business, Eve got educated on how to manage a company by the seat of her pants—learning as she went. Six years later, she had built a seven figure business.

Then the world changed.

Crushing News—Home and the World

Jake was diagnosed with juvenile diabetes and her attention turned to managing the disease and helping them adapt to a new life of regular monitoring, medication, and doctor's visits.

As a single mom, she took time away from work to assist Jake, hoping that her staff could manage without her. A month later, problems began to arise and Eve was torn between work and home.

Then the other shoe fell—9/11. The world seemed to stop. People were in shock from the terrorist attacks. No one could work. Clients cancelled appointments which left large gaps in their schedule.

Although she had strong sales people and good trainers, it was Eve who the clients wanted. The company always showcased Eve as their star. When she had to take time away from work, it caused many problems.

As a business owner, you can predict when some challenges may arise, but then there are the ones that creep up and surprise you, such as 9/11 did. Still,

Eve did not rush back to the office. Jake's diagnosis was new and they were still building a system to manage it.

The Pile-Up

Problems confront entrepreneurs daily. Gently brushing up against us or shoving us suddenly from behind, they take us off course; changing our focus from forward movement to putting out the present fire. Dependant upon the severity of the problem will either allow us to move quickly through it or struggle to get grounded.

With the physical absence of Eve, the weaker links, the ones Eve *would get to when she had time*, grew weaker.

For instance, Eve was deciding on vendors for a new computer system. She had spoken to many of them, but eventually chose her top two. The more expensive vendor wanted $50,000 to do the job. He was also going to throw in extensive follow-up training on the system and a two-year warranty. She liked that. The other vendor was new in business and wanted to win this deal. He charged $30,000. He appeared very conscientious and had gotten great reviews by other business owners. This second vendor was not throwing in any warranties or training on the system.

She tossed and turned many sleepless nights trying to make the right decision. Although she was leaning toward the *soup to nuts* vendor, the $50,000 one, Eve put off the decision for months because it was a big purchase, and she didn't have the time to give it concentrated thought.

Another nagging issue was the receptionist. She greeted the clients, chatted with them while they waited for the trainers, got them coffee, and answered the phones. She was also supposed to keep the reception area neat. But many times since she had been hired, Eve had to remind her of these responsibilities. She wondered why she couldn't remember. It wasn't as if the receptionist was swamped. If she got distracted talking to people, she'd just forget to answer the phones. Of course, this was a real problem. Missed calls were missed opportunities. During this time especially, they couldn't afford to neglect new business opportunities or lose clients.

Eve knew that the receptionist needed better training. Although she meant to get around to it, she never did. Nor did she get around to assigning someone to work with her.

"Maybe in the back of my mind, I'm not sure she's worth training," she thought.

She couldn't let this go on forever. Eve had to make a decision about her.

She always told herself, "There were more pressing matters to tend to."

Something close to Eve's heart had also fallen through the cracks. It was the after-hours mentoring program. As a former teacher, it was very important to Eve that her staff volunteered time at some of the inner city after school programs. Or they could choose to do some volunteer work at the Boys & Girls Club of America. However, no one in their office was managing this project and only one person had volunteered. Another gap in her world.

CLARITY

Many of us just don't know what to do when we're faced with a large challenge. I suggest when you're grinding about a difficult situation to suspend any decision making for the moment. Instead create a transition for your thoughts. Stop the track you're currently on.

Here's what you can do. Envision a peaceful resting place, like a garden or mountain top. Rest brings peace. That's just what you want to create in order to bring clarity to your problem. Clarity allows you to see more resources. It helps bring to light, with less grinding and more ease, just what is needed. You can also do this resting time at others periods, such as when you're in an argument. Just step away from the argument for the moment. Let the person know you'll be back to them shortly, but that you can't continue this argument right now.

Music also has its resting places. You can hear them in every piece of music or song. Imagine the beauty of music with its highlight on the richness of the notes. There is also beauty in the silence between the notes (the resting place). For without that silence, the notes would not hold their richness. There would just be a continual blending of endless sound. It is the silence between the notes, however short, that creates the beauty of the music we hear.

Claude Debussy, the French composer said, "Music is actually the silence between the notes."

So it is in business. The place of rest gives us a chance to renew, see things from a fresh perspective. It brings us clarity. It can bring quality and value to our work.

Rewards from Clarity

Eve was a resourceful woman. Concerned about the decrease in revenue, she kept a positive outlook, as if *knowing* it would turn out fine. Because she could compartmentalize worry, she was able to take advantage of the slow-down in business. She was a hands-on, *in-your-face* business leader. Now she needed to find a way to manage her company from home for the next few months. She had never done this before and had no model to follow.

She arranged an outing with her whole team. They closed the office for a day and did some team building exercises. The team building was seamless and people were laughing and collaborating on the activities. This was a good sign.

Next Eve gathered her team in a circle. It was time for the main event. Because she had been able to step away from the problems, she had more clarity. Instead of trying to come up with all the answers herself, she used the afternoon to have the team list some of the issues they were facing and then brainstorm ideas. It was a simple, but brilliant process. Including her team in identifying challenges and creating solutions brought them closer together. There was no grinding, no panic. At the end of the day, the team came up with the idea to designate someone as the go-between leader while Eve worked from home.

As for the computer vendor, Eve had set up an appointment to close the deal with the $50,000 vendor when she came back from leave. Upon her return, she met him in her office for the appointed time set. She was about to sign on the dotted line, when suddenly she stopped. It was if a small child was tugging on her sleeve wanting attention. Because she was practicing clarity, she could actually sense this tugging. It came from her gut and told her not to sign with him. Even though the deal was almost done, and even though she had set up this appointment, and even though he was in front of her right now, she looked up and told the vendor that she had made a mistake.

Eve called the merchant who was charging $30,000 and signed with him. Three weeks later the $50,000 vendor went out of business. Had she done business with his company she could have lost money and not gotten a system.

ASK YOURSELF

These questions will help you get in touch with your inner voice. Then apply the following practices. The more you practice, the more connected you will get with your best friend and your greatest advisor—you.

1. What (tough) decision(s) am I currently facing?
2. What are my choices?
3. What do I need to make my decision?
4. When was the last time I had a gut feeling about something and it was right?
5. What happened?
6. When was the last time I had a gut feeling about something and it was wrong?
7. What happened?
8. What do I want (or need) to learn today?

PRACTICE THIS

When you become skilled at listening to your inner guidance system, you will make decisions on a new, often exhilarating level. If you haven't relied on your intuition in the past, it may feel like a leap of faith. Like you're jumping into an ice cold river in the dead of winter—shocking and frightening. All types of questions may come up:

Is this really my voice I'm hearing?
What is this voice trying to tell me?
How about if I follow this voice, and it is wrong?

You may question why you're listening to this advice, especially if you've never attempted this before or if you can't see the outcome.

Inside each of us is this subtle voice, our inner guidance. It is barely audible, and can easily go unheard, especially if we're grinding on the problem, or even listening to the advice of others. Call it instinct, intuition, a sixth sense, or your gut, this is your inner voice—your inner guidance system—your advisor.

Connecting to it is an innate ability that takes conscious practice in order to actually hear it. The more you practice, the better you'll recognize it. You'll be able to use your inner guidance system more often. Here are some effective practices to turn up the volume.

Practice #1: Stop, Breathe, Relax . . . Now

Many years ago I worked with a meditation teacher. He used four words to get people grounded at times of anxiety, fear, stress, depression, and sadness. Not only do I still use these words on a continual basis myself, but I teach them to many of my clients. These words will bring you back to your center.

> Stop.
> Breathe.
> Relax.
> Now.

Stop

First *stop* what you are doing. For instance, if you're driving and someone cuts you off in traffic, instead of getting angry, turning red, and flipping them the middle finger, stop your thoughts. I know this can be difficult. The desire to brew or stay angry when an injustice is done to us is our typical human response.

It is easier when just starting out with this practice to displace yourself from what just happened. Pull off the road if you can. It will be for just a moment. Bring yourself away from what just happened and get into the present.

Once you can stop those thoughts, you are healing, not doing emotional and physical injury to yourself. Hatred and resentment can eat you up and create physical problems like stomach-aches, headaches, or worse.

There is a Zen story of two monks, which I have applied to many contexts, especially while driving. It helps with road rage. As you read it, consider a time when you held on to anger or resentment and how that made you feel.

Two traveling monks reached a river where they met a young woman dressed in fine silk apparel. Wary of the current, she asked if they would carry her across to other side of the river so she didn't get her dress wet.

One of the monks hesitated, but the other quickly picked her up onto his shoulders, transported her across the water, and put her down on the other bank. She thanked him and departed.

The monk who had hesitated said to the very wet monk, "You shouldn't have done that. It's against our rules to touch a woman."

The wet monk said what's done is done, so just get over it. As the monks continued on their way, the one (monk) was brooding and preoccupied. Unable to hold his silence, he spoke out.

"Brother, our spiritual training teaches us to avoid any contact with women, but you picked that one up on your shoulders and carried her!"

"Brother," the second monk replied, "I set her down on the other side, while you are still carrying her."

Like the second monk, there is no need to carry resentment. You can let it go. But first you must stop and notice it.

Breathe

The second step is to *breathe*. Take some deep breaths. Breathing calms us down. Taking in oxygen will help to release tension. If you've pulled your car over, or even if you're still driving, you can do this. Breathing is a great, natural relaxant—and it costs nothing and has no side effects, except feeling good.

Just remember what L. Frank Baum, the author of *The Wonderful Wizard of Oz* said, "Whenever I feel blue, I start breathing again."

Relax

Next, *relax*. Focus on your shoulders and neck. Let your shoulders drop down and move your neck side to side and up and down. Notice where you are holding tension. Is it in your hand, your stomach, your lower back? Wherever it may be, focus there as you breathe into it. Do this until you feel more relaxed.

Now

Lastly is *now*. Now means getting present—coming into the moment. Come back, away from your disappointment or resentment, to the present. You give up thinking about what just happened or what could happen.

Fretting about the past or future creates more stress. Being in the present, the *now*, creates peace of mind.

These four steps take very little time. They can be done in a minute, maybe even seconds. When you begin to utilize this four step process, you will not only relax, but you'll also clear your mind. You can't hear your inner voice when your mind is cluttered with noise.

Practice #2: In the Silence, Listen Closely

Once the clutter and noise is gone, you'll be able to hear your inner guidance. Throw out a question to the universe and to yourself.

Questions I ask regularly are, "What would you like me to hear or see? What is my next step?"

Ask the questions regularly, upon waking and before going to sleep are best. It's not uncommon to wake up with more clarity. Overnight the messages can seep in and marinate awhile before the tasks of the day crowd them out. When you're sleeping, the barriers are down and it is easier to receive your inner wisdom.

If you're awake and it's during the day, find a quiet spot and get silent before asking your question. You won't want the busyness of the day to distract you from *hearing* the answers. There's no need to ask the question out loud. You can ask it silently. Promise yourself that you'll remain open to receive all signs and signals from your inner guide.

Each day, find an opportunity to listen to your inner voice.

If you aren't facing any major issues or decisions to be made, then go ahead and create some new growth for yourself by asking: *What is it that you want me to learn today?* You are on your way to opening up a new source for wise answers. Don't try to interpret these answers. Just trust them.

Practice #3: Trust Yourself First

When you hear your inner voice, at first it will be just a feeling, maybe just a twinge. You may even miss it if you're not paying close attention. Or you may dismiss it, thinking it sounds silly, impractical, or even unrealistic.

The more uncluttered your mind, the better able you'll be to hear. Think of a room full of people shouting, while one person is trying to talk. It's hard to hear that person until the shouting and noise stops. When there's no interference, listening for your internal guidance becomes easy.

You'll probably ask yourself, "Can I trust what I'm hearing?"

Only you can answer that. The best way is to test it out. Try it on a not-so-important decision. Gradually build up to the tougher ones. At first it may sound illogical. That's fine. It's like hearing a baby cry in the nursery. You have to get used to the sound of your baby's cry to differentiate it from the others. My inner voice has never steered me wrong. I have come to trust it.

Here is what Oprah Winfrey has to say about this in her 2008 commencement speech at Stanford University:

> How do you know when you're doing something right? How do you know that? It feels so. What I know now is that feelings are really your GPS system for life. When you're supposed to do something or not supposed to do something, your emotional guidance system lets you know. The trick is to learn to check your ego at the door and start checking your gut instead. Every right decision I've made—has come from my gut. And every wrong

decision I've ever made was a result of me not listening to the greater voice of myself.

If it doesn't feel right, don't do it. That's the lesson. And that lesson alone will save you, my friends, a lot of grief. Even doubt means don't. This is what I've learned. There are many times when you don't know what to do. When you don't know what to do, get still, get very still, until you do know what to do.

And when you do get still and let your internal motivation be the driver, not only will your personal life improve, but you will gain a competitive edge in the working world as well. Because, as Daniel Pink writes in his best-seller, *A Whole New Mind*, we're entering a whole new age. And he calls it the Conceptual Age, where traits that set people apart today are going to come from our hearts—right brain—as well as our heads.[1]

SUMMARY

- ☑ Your inner voice speaks loudest when you're sleeping. Ask a question before you fall asleep.
- ☑ Ask the same question upon rising in the morning.
- ☑ Take time each day to get quiet and listen to your inner voice.
- ☑ The more you practice listening and attending to it, the more it will become your trusted guide.
- ☑ Start by asking questions on matters that aren't that important. Build up to tougher ones.
- ☑ Your inner voice can guide you to the next step in the direction you want to go.
- ☑ Stop, Breathe, Relax, Now.
- ☑ It's all about trust.

NOTE

1. A. Gorlick, "Oprah Winfrey addresses Stanford Class of 2008," Stanford University News, Stanford Report, June 15, 2008.

12

Give Yourself a Standing O

Every moment of your life is infinitely creative and the universe is endlessly bountiful. Just put forth a clear enough request, and everything your heart desires must come to you.[1]

Mahatma Gandhi

HONOR THYSELF

Being appreciated is a wonderful feeling—inspiring and quite motivating. Frederick Herzberg, a psychologist recognized for his motivational theory in business management, found that giving praise or acknowledgment for an employee's excellent work is the primary motivation for continued good performance. It is a higher-level motivator than money.[1]

For the entrepreneur, part of his job description is to rouse employees, vendors, and support people to perform well. But who lends praise and recognition to motivate the person at the top—the isolated entrepreneur?

After speaking to many entrepreneurs, I noticed they rarely gave themselves a *way-to-go* or standing ovation for a job well done. Seems trite you may say. It's not. Read on.

Disconnected

Brendan was that man at the top. He had been running a chain of laundromats and dry cleaning businesses for two decades. He loved to work and did it well. Every year his revenues nearly doubled. People in the community respected him and employees rarely left on their own. He was generous with praise and rewarded good work. Brendan was also charitable and donated large sums of money to fight illiteracy.

Life as Brendan knew it was good; however, something was missing inside. No one would have believed that he felt like a hollow shell—the exterior looked perfect, but the interior was empty.

Brendan didn't hire me to help grow his business or increase his income. Although the two would be the beneficiaries of his work with me. Instead he wanted to investigate this void feeling. He claimed he had no reason to feel this way, since anyone looking at his life would want to be him. Yet he just wasn't happy.

On the move continually, his to-do list was his motivator, committed to memory—telling him which tasks had to be done and by when. He'd complete a task and then move on to the next. If he had success, he'd shrug it off to *that's the way it should be done.* He never stopped, even momentarily, to silently slap himself with a high-five for a job well done. According to Brendan there was not much time to stand still and do anything that wasn't productive. Occasionally he would reward himself for hard work with a monetary gift—a dividend from his business, a sailboat, or a BMW convertible. But the thrill of those wore off quickly as it does with the attainment of most material objects.

Days blended together, one day moving into the next as if there was not a line of delineation as the midnight hour struck. Brendan was a disconnected man—disconnected from himself. This was the main cause for the void he felt deep inside.

The Importance of Appreciation

Brendan didn't believe in self-acknowledgment. He came from a family of blue collar workers who knew the value of hard work. His parents never complained about, nor acknowledged, their labor. They just did it—no appreciation, just something that had to get done. Herzberg stated that appreciation is a motivator that taps into your energy supply—creating more power and desire to perform well—the value of receiving it being immeasurable. Brendan had no clue that this was missing, or that it should even be present.

Uncomfortable when others would congratulate him, he would simply shrug his shoulders and wave his hand as if saying *don't say that, it wasn't such a big deal.* He never had a passing thought of being grateful for something he accomplished. And appearing self-centered was the last thing he wanted. In this respect he was like many entrepreneurs, including myself in the past. Too busy to stop and take the time to acknowledge what they achieve.

As Brendan explored this empty feeling, he got in touch with his life and how meaningless it felt. This made him sad and confused. He had a great income, a successful business, loyal employees, and a wonderful family. He supported the community and a nonprofit cause. How could his life be meaningless? He was doing more than most people ever do?

When I asked Brendan, "Why do you do what you do?" He paused. He couldn't answer.

Finally, he said, "My days look the same, except for a different meeting or project. After all, what I do is just help people get their clothes clean. That's nothing so great in the world. It's not like I'm discovering a cure for cancer."

MO—MODUS OPERANDI

Something big was missing, something significant—something almost every entrepreneur faces at one time or another. Brendan couldn't see his future. He had nothing that really excited him, motivated, made him get up in the morning. Sure, he liked what he did, but it lacked meaning and purpose. Brendan didn't have an MO or a *modus operandi*, or what I define as a reason to do what you do.

The Starbucks Way

Granted, getting someone's clothes clean isn't a big deal. But Brendan was missing the point. He did more than that. People dropped off their clothes before they went to work or on their way home. Sometimes his employees were the first people their customers saw that day and perhaps the last they saw at the end of the day. They had an opportunity to make an impact, helping them to start or end their days feeling good.

Starbucks got it right. They sell coffee. And they sell some food, not much food, and not always the right kind of food. But if you ask the founder, Howard Schultz, he'll tell you what they sell are coffee and an entire experience. A cozy experience with music playing and the smell of coffee permeating the air as soon as you open the door, it always puts me in a good mood

Brendan didn't get it. He was selling clean clothes. But that wasn't it at all. He was really selling attitude, the opportunity to impact people positively.

As we discussed this over a cup of coffee at Starbucks, something clicked with Brendan. He took out a pad of paper and wrote for a half hour nonstop. Then he looked up and smiled.

"I got it!"

He let out such a deep heartfelt laugh as his eyes filled with tears. Brendan had made a discovery.

Filling the Void

He jumped up from the table and told me he had to go outside. In the parking lot he let out a loud WOO-HOO and laughed, slapping the air with high-fives as he jumped.

People came into his stores daily. They were all ages—lonely looking elderly folks who had lost their close friends, frazzled young mothers pushing strollers, and business people on cell phones—tense and impatient as though everyone was an obstacle to get what they needed.

"A laundromat and dry cleaners is what we give people, like coffee for Starbucks," Brendan said.

"I've always felt empty inside with this business. Yeah, I make great money, but there's still this hole in me. I think I finally got it. Shultz created an atmosphere to take people away from their daily grind. My company makes people feel good. We can have coffee, lollipops, and dog biscuits.

I can bring someone in to help train my people on creating exceptional customer service—and it's not just saying please and thank you. It's more. I want people to leave my store feeling listened to. They start their day dropping off their clothes and then pick them up at the end of the day. We really can have an impact on how their day begins and ends."

Brendan was on a roll. He saw that to bring excitement to anything, even cleaning clothes, he had to find the purpose behind it all. He claimed his purpose in that moment and never looked back. He would make sure that every employee learned to listen to their customers and treated them with kindness.

It was simple, so simple that at first he couldn't believe it. If he could help people feel happier in the world, where the news was always so dreadful, it made him feel good.

"Who knows," he said. "Maybe my customers will then go pass on the good vibes to others."

This excited him even more.

A new car, a high definition TV, or another play toy is a fine reward for good work. No one in their right mind would deny the fact that having the money to buy whatever you want is a great thing. But that's not what fuels our work because the excitement of a prize is short-lived. After the thrill of having a material thing wears off, the void returns. Finding the purpose or meaning behind what you do is where the richness lies. For example, I help people to build successful businesses. And that is just a fantastic role. But even better, as they build a successful business they also build a successful life. Now that's a homerun. It's what keeps me coming back over and over again to help people.

Rise to Your Feet in Honor

Finding your purpose is finding your MO. It gives meaning to what you do. When you identify your MO, you'll feel more compassion than ever before. And you won't want to stop. You'll have bigger shoes to fill then just doing your *job*. You will have more meaning in your work (and your life). You'll feel prouder, and more passionate and excited about your work.

Most leaders have bought into the myth that you must have a calloused skin to run a business. True, the entrepreneur's path is one of many landmines, but that doesn't mean you need to shut down and move mindlessly from task to task. Once you know your MO, you'll move through your daily accomplishments with greater appreciation.

Appreciation can be expressed with a silent pat on the back, a smile, a song you sing, the *happy* dance, or a standing O (O for ovation). When you can appreciate and acknowledge yourself, you'll have the tools to also do the same for others. The difference now is that other people will really get your sincerity.

Standing O versus Ego-Stroking

Giving yourself a standing O for a job well done opens up the heart. It brings you into the present moment to take a brief look at what you have accomplished and the benefits it brings. A standing O comes from self-appreciation and is a generous gesture of self-care. You are taking care of yourself by acknowledging the work that you've done. It is for you only, nothing that has to be shared with another.

Ego-stroking builds you up in front of others because internally, and perhaps unconsciously, you don't feel adequate, capable, powerful, or worthy. Ego-stroking is out to prove how great you are.

It is the exceptional and secure person who takes time to acknowledge and appreciate his accomplishments and it sure is fun to do it with a standing O. For instance, at the end of a great performance, you are moved to your feet through the energy of the room, clapping, waving your arms in the air, stamping your feet, cheering, and whistling to acknowledge the performers on stage. When was the last time you did that for yourself?

There are four practices that will help you to create the self-motivating act of appreciation in the form of a standing O. But first let's start with some questions to ask yourself, and then I'll define the steps for you.

ASK YOURSELF

Take some quality time to get quiet, close your eyes, and ask yourself these questions. You may have to mull the questions around for awhile before you can find the answers. It's fine to ask the question and go about your day with it in the back of your mind. Sometimes answers come to me best this way.

---

1. Do you always feel fulfilled in your work?
2. Do you know your MO? If so, what is it?
3. Does your MO motivate you? If not, it probably isn't your true MO.
4. When was the last time you gave yourself a standing O or some other form of self acknowledgment?
5. What often stops you from giving yourself a standing O?

PRACTICE THIS

Practice #1: Describe Your MO

Your MO is what makes your juices flow, what makes you do what you do, what motivates and excites you. Like Brendan, when you haven't identified it, you may feel dulled or empty by your work. Identifying your MO will bring excitement. You'll anticipate more the joy in the day ahead.

First, know that identifying your MO can take some time. So don't get frustrated, just stay with it. Next, make a list of what you are passionate about. It could be as simple as taking walks in autumn. Or, it could be fighting for a cause, such as ending world hunger. Then circle three items on your list that are your top passions. Notice if they have anything in common. For instance, if you circled: listening to beautiful music, walks in autumn, and helping people to be the best they can be (these are some of mine), then look to see if any of them interconnect.

Listening to music helps me get into my soul. I begin to feel at peace, grounded. Walks also do the same for me. And when I witness people stretching and expanding in who they are, I am connected to the internal power that we all have—as if our hearts are speaking to each other.

Your top three things will also be connected, but you'll have to identify them first.

When you have completed this step, write down your statement. Let's use mine as an example.

My purpose is helping people feel successful and powerful.

Don't worry if doesn't sound perfect or if you think there is a better one inside of you. For now, this is a great start. So let's give you a standing O for identifying your MO.

Practice #2: Separate Appreciation from Your Ego

Appreciation of yourself and stroking your ego are two separate acts. Appreciation is not something you need to boast about to others. However, your ego may want to. For 21 days don't tell anyone how great you are, what you've accomplished, or what you will accomplish. Instead let your MO drive your work. Appreciate your accomplishments silently by some standing O's. You'll want to tell others. Don't. See how it feels to keep this appreciation to yourself. You may want to burst open if you don't tell someone. Stay with that feeling a while and don't give in to it. Instead, silently acknowledge yourself or even write it down. Then, go notice what someone else has done—and acknowledge them out loud instead.

Practice #3: When No One Is Looking, Stand Up and Cheer

When you are by yourself, you can get crazy with appreciation for what you've done. I want you to do that. Do the happy dance. Sing. Shout. Laugh. You're doing something unbelievable in this world by being an entrepreneur who is not only building a business but also has a purpose behind it. So celebrate!

Practice #4: Bask in Your Own Glory, Then Get Back to Work

Once you've done the happy dance or given yourself a standing O, move on. You can continue to appreciate yourself, but keep it in the background now. Get back to your MO. Sometimes basking in glory too long can sidetrack you. Set up a time period that looks like this. Take a half-hour walk and smile as you crunch on leaves, laughing as you appreciate yourself for who you are and what you've just accomplished. Then after that half hour get back to what you're up to. That walk or standing O will light the way for what's next.

Awkward at first, self-appreciation filters into your energy source and fuels it—making any short-lived moments of accomplishment feel last a lot longer. This not only feels good, but keeps you in that zone where anything is possible. A standing O is not a luxury or even an option. It is the restorative key to that deep source of omnipresent, positive energy within.

You're becoming more conscious. You're becoming a more conscious entrepreneur. Congratulations!

SUMMARY

- ☑ Work is more then doing tasks and making money.
- ☑ Satisfying work comes from knowing your MO—modus operandi.
- ☑ Appreciate yourself often with a standing O.
- ☑ Put your ego to sleep and don't acknowledge yourself in front of others. Instead acknowledge someone else.
- ☑ Bask silently in your glory.
- ☑ Then get back to work, taking the energy from your personal standing O that will light your way.

NOTE

1. Frederick Herzberg, *One More Time: How Do You Motivate Employees?* (Boston: Harvard Business Press, 2008).

13

Growing Strong

It's not about how to achieve your dreams. It's about how to lead your life.
If you lead your life the right way, the karma will take care of itself. The
dreams will come to you.

Randy Pausch, *The Last Lecture*

There isn't an entrepreneur that wouldn't want to be in JJ's shoes. His company
was on the fast track for growth and he was producing double digit profits. But
growth brings its own problems. The buyers who bought JJ's business would
put him through the ringers. In the end, he would need to question how he
wanted to live the rest of his life. JJ's story is a testament to an entrepreneur
who became successful, sold his company, and made a decision that would
impact the lives of many.

RAGS TO RICHES

JJ grew up in the south—in a small back woods town. His parents were
poor and the family lived in a one bedroom house with no electricity. JJ shared
the bedroom with his three brothers. His parents slept in the living room-
kitchen area. He was up before dawn to work on the farm before walking
to school, which was a two-mile trek each way. When his alarm went off at
5:00 a.m., he would grimace. Getting up early was never something that he
would get used to. The shrill sound of the alarm in the silence of the dark, cold
house made him bury his head further under the covers.

Rain or shine, he had jobs to do as he forced himself out of bed. Before
breakfast he would feed the horse and hogs, clean the hen cage and collect
their eggs, shovel straw for the cows to eat, and wash down the outhouse.
By 6:00 a.m., he was cleaned up and sitting at the breakfast table with his family, gulping down eggs and trying to remember what he had to bring to school
that day.

JJ knew he was destined for a better life. He waited for the day he gradu-
ated high school and would be able to leave the place he called home. Unlike
many of the local boys who never completed school and ended up on the

streets or in jail, JJ was bright and had a burning desire to be something in life. While other kids were getting into trouble after class, JJ was in the school's library reading and doing his homework.

Dr. Loughton

JJ's wish came true. He packed up and left home as he headed for college. He would never return to the place he called home again. One of his professors was impressed with his work ethic and took JJ under his guidance. In turn, JJ would always be grateful for the path that Dr. Loughton started him down.

Loughton taught finance at the university and also had a side-line investment business. He had made fortunes for himself and others. People from all over the world clamored to Loughton's door for advice or to become his next client to grow a strong portfolio. As his investment business grew, Loughton hired other advisors to help serve his clientele. Teaching was a way for the professor to give back, an opportunity to impact and influence some of his students with high potential. JJ was one of them.

Loughton opened up the world of business to JJ. He taught him about finance, sales, and success. He also taught him about the power of integrity in business.

"Being true to yourself and your own principles and values will always come back to support you," he shared with JJ.

"Contrarily, if you don't follow your beliefs, and you listen to popular opinions instead, it will come back to haunt you," he stated.

Loughton not only influenced how JJ thought, but he gave him an opportunity to make money. His investment company faced the challenge most companies face—getting qualified sales leads. Because Loughton's business was expanding with new advisors, he needed an avenue to bring leads to his team. Enter JJ, the technology whiz kid.

During his senior year, he took on the project to assist Loughton. By graduation he had developed a successful system to generate qualified lead-flow.

Loughton brought JJ on full-time. JJ put together a team of people in India and the United States to assist with the operation of lead flow. It was complicated, but according to Loughton, JJ had it up and running in a short period of time with minimal glitches.

Five years later, JJ was hungry for more, but Loughton had decided that this was the point where he'd take his company—no further. He was getting up in years and his energy was not like it used to be. The company had grown well beyond anything that he could have ever imagined. He was sitting on a small fortune for retirement.

After a year of discussions to buy Loughton out or to go find another company to work for, they both agreed that JJ should go start his own company. Loughton was ready to pare down, but didn't want to sell his business yet.

As a parting gift, he gave JJ full rights to the lead generation technology that he had created. JJ was ready to start up his own company.

Out of the Garage

JJ had little savings. He was renting a small home near the beach with a couple of other ex-classmates. There was no space inside to set up an office, or even a desk for a phone and computer. He cleared out the garage which was used as a dumping ground for storage and junk, gave it a paint job, bought a used desk and a computer, registered his company's name with the state, and was ready for business. He kept his connections in India and hired two young geeks with experience of doing business in America. They were as hungry as JJ and told him they'd invest in building this company by not getting a large salary until the company was rolling in cash. Then they'd expect a return on their *investment*. Things were going well.

The problems that many start-up entrepreneurs face eluded JJ. He seemed to have the golden touch. He was in the right industry at the right time with little overhead.

As more people were turned away from corporate America, they sought out new paths of work. Many took self-education courses to open up consulting businesses. A good percentage entered the investment field, which was wide open for new investors. Ka-ching! They needed sales. JJ's company was positioned to offer them leads.

Within two years, he had outgrown his *office space* in the garage and moved to real office space. Before moving, his three full-time employees shared a desk and computer. Now they each had their own cubicle with a desk and computer. JJ felt proud.

GOING FOR THE GOLD

Although his Internet marketing business in Los Angeles grew stronger and stronger, he never forgot his back woods roots. The days of sharing a small bedroom with his brothers were far behind him in years, but not in memory.

He got involved in Junior Achievement (JA), the world's largest organization dedicated to educating students about workforce readiness, entrepreneurship, and financial literacy through experiential, hands-on programs. JA programs help prepare young people for the real world by showing them how to generate wealth and effectively manage it.[1]

As his company grew, he wanted to give back. JA was the perfect outlet for him.

JJ's company was grossing $12 million. He managed 15 employees around the world. He told friends that if he played his cards right, he'd have a personal savings of $1 million within five years.

He was wrong.

He had $6 million in three years.

Surprise Call

JJ took the call from the chief operating officer of a competing company. They were Goliath to JJ's David. The interested company was publicly traded and grossed $500 million last year. They continued to grow by 10 percent annually.

Nathan began the phone call with a compliment in a southern drawl.

"We've been watching you, son. You sure are growing that company of yours. I'm not going to beat around the bush, son, we're impressed—everyone from the president to the executive team. I'd like to come out and meet you and personally shake your hand. I'm coming to L.A. in a day and wondered if you wouldn't mind joining me for breakfast at the City Club on Bunker Hill?"

JJ's mouth dropped open. Was he dreaming?

Nathan said, "Then maybe you can show me around your operation."

Stunned, he tried to move his mouth and words wouldn't come out. He sipped on some water. Somewhere in the back of his mind he knew he'd eventually sell the company. But he wasn't prepared for the timing of this call. Plus—an invitation for breakfast at the elite City Club, the club he had been trying to get into, was too much to fathom.

Meeting with Nathan

Weeks after they met, Nathan called him on the phone once again. This time he told JJ that his company wanted to make him a strong offer to buy his company. JJ had tossed numbers around in his head for weeks, preparing for this follow up call from Nathan. Anything lower than three million dollars he wouldn't take. He argued for both in his mind—selling the business or not. Money won out. If Nathan came back and offered him $3 million, he'd sign tomorrow.

No one knew about the initial meeting with Nathan. Not even his management team. No need to mention this until things got serious. Until then, he wanted everyone's attention where it belonged—on their jobs.

The Offer

The offer floored JJ. He couldn't get his mind around this type of number. Nathan offered to buy the company on these conditions. JJ would initially get $3 million upfront. He would be required to stay for 18 months as president and keep his team in place as best as he could. They expected to see similar current day profits over this period of time. He would receive a salary and benefits. They would continue to pick up all of his expenses as if he were still the owner of the company. At the end of the 18 months, if he increased profits they would give him a bonus based on a sliding scale. JJ would be expected to train his replacement, who would more than likely come from the parent company. Upon his exit and if all proceeded along the stated terms, he would be given another $3 million paid out over 15 months.

JJ wanted to jump through the phone and give Nathan a great big hand-shake to close the deal. Instead JJ calmly told him that he needed to think about it.

Nathan said, "You have one week, son. The deal is non-negotiable. Then we pull the deal off the table. Think long and hard about this."

A Different Kind of Pressure

Most entrepreneurs feel the pressure of making payroll, expansion, profit-ability, employee, customer, or operations issues. JJ would tell you he could not remember having that type of pressure. His business sky-rocketed from day one, then stayed in the stratosphere throughout the acquisition. The stressful decisions that entrepreneurs faced daily were foreign to him. Per-haps some of those stressors really were there, but JJ's attitude didn't let it affect him. Either way, this was all new to him.

He couldn't sleep that entire week. On the seventh day, he called Nathan and accepted the offer as is. The agreement was in his lawyer's hands hours later.

THE MANAGEMENT TEAM

The problem started the moment JJ told his team. There was Salvatore who headed up IT, Will who headed up operations, Taylor who headed up sales, and Callie in finance and human resources. Four in total.

The team was shocked. This was unexpected news. Immediately they questioned why JJ hadn't let them in on this from the beginning. He was pre-pared and answered honestly that he was unsure of the direction it would take. He didn't want to take them off track. He had their best interests at heart and would be sure they were taken care of. JJ needed them more then ever. He would see to it that they could either stay with the parent company once he left, or be given a very generous bonus upon exiting.

The team stayed intact.

The Exit

He got a taste of corporate America. JJ had to learn to break through the red tape to get a decision he could make in seconds. Then there was the brown-nosing that turned his stomach. Couldn't people see through that? Competition in the new company was fierce. People cowed down to the boss, and lost them-selves in the process. Titles and status ruled.

There were advantages. With lots of money, you can call the shots. And they did. Vendors lowered prices, people lined up to work for them, and salaries, benefits, and stock options were quite remarkable.

JJ kept his commitment. His management team drove the numbers and he was the conduit between his company and the parent. JJ had been in negotiations for almost the entire 18 months with the parent company. He wanted large bonuses for the management team members who chose to leave at the end of their tenure.

JJ tried to set them up for life. He wanted them to walk away from this deal with a large retirement package. But the parent company was not buying it. Even promising a longer term of employment by his team until the successful transition had been made, failed. JJ was distraught. He had promised his employees. Now he couldn't deliver. Looking back, he realized he had jumped the gun. JJ had not taken this into consideration as part of the deal. He assumed it would happen because he requested it.

The Decision

None of the team stayed longer than their committed dates. The new culture was different and they struggled with it. Their old entrepreneurial environment had turned into a behemoth giant. It was not what they had signed up for. They turned to JJ for their promised bonuses. He looked into their eyes and knew that he had to make a decision. He couldn't let them down, not after everything they had done for him. The parent company had refused larger bonuses. All they offered was one year's salary and outplacement services. To most people this would have been fine. But not to JJ.

He sweetened the pot. JJ took his $6 million buy-out and gave each one of them $1 million. He walked away with $2 million. He made millionaires out of each one of them.

They couldn't believe what he had done. No one would have done this. Any other CEO would have taken the $6 million and run with it, leaving them each with one year's salary payout. JJ had integrity and a promise was a promise. Born dirt poor didn't mean that the family who raised him didn't have strong values. He had learned much from them.

What Happened Next

JJ signed a non-compete agreement when he sold the business. For two years, he could not open or operate a competing business within 100 miles of his old operation. JJ did not work for another two years. His team members searched for another company and a boss like the one they had just left. They couldn't find one. Every so often they'd all get together for dinner and talk about the old days, reminiscing about how much fun it was, especially in the first couple of years. What would it be like, they wondered to try to do it again?

Two years later, they each took their investment and opened up a company together. Even though JJ's non-compete agreement had come to term, the thought of opening another company similar to the old one was too difficult a thought.

They changed gears and started up a bank. With many banking joint venture relationships and strong networks in the financial field, they were primed for another successful venture.

In the wake of JJ's successful first run, they started up another company that grew quickly. JJ now had four partners, all investors. He owned the majority share of 75 percent of the company and had the final decision on all major matters. Several years later, their bank was sold to another Goliath.

Present Day

Today JJ has retired from the business world, or so he says. He teaches business courses to entrepreneurs and does some investing. Loughton passed away years before JJ's retirement, but JJ knows that his mentor would have been quite proud of him. When asked why he gave the management team so much money out of his own pocket, he says, "When I look in the mirror, I can smile back at my image, thinking, this is a good man."

ASK YOURSELF

Good begets good. Just look at JJ. He passed on millions of dollars to the people who stood by his side and helped him to build his dream. When the acquiring company refused to recognize his key employees, JJ didn't have to think long about what needed to be done. He didn't do it expecting anything in return. But returns he got. His employees invested their millions in a new company with JJ. It made them all millionaires many times over.

Doing what is right by your own standards, doesn't always end up like it did for JJ. That's not the sole reason to do it. Perhaps the real reason is what JJ stated. You can look in the mirror and smile, instead of having to turn away.

Take some quality time to get quiet, close your eyes, and ask yourself these questions.

1. What are five standards that you abide by in your life and work?
2. Recall a time when one of these standards was in question? What did you do?
3. Recall a time when you went against one of your standards. What was the outcome? How did that make you feel both emotionally and physically?
4. Is there someone that you'd like to reward monetarily, but hesitate?
5. Have you ever given someone something that went beyond their wildest expectations? What was that process like for you? How did you feel?
6. Have you ever received something from someone that went beyond your wildest expectations? What did you do with it?

PRACTICE THIS

If you've got systems in place in your company, the right people onboard, and strong advisors, yet you're still wondering why your business is flat or growth is slow, then follow these practices. They may bring a new dimension to you and your business. Perhaps you will be the next JJ.

Practice #1: Vision Board

When I was younger and lived in an apartment, I had a walk-in closet. I covered the inside walls of that closet with pictures of my dreams—everything I wanted for my life. I got very specific. There were cut out pictures of houses—interiors and exteriors. I posted a picture of a magnificent multi-leveled deck that looked over the ocean. I could smell the ocean every time I looked at it.

I also cut out pictures of my dream kitchen, cars I wanted to drive, relationships I wanted to have, and pictures of who I wanted to be and what I wanted to do. I wanted to be successful, so there was a picture that represented that. I wanted to travel, so there were pictures of where I wanted to travel.

This is a very powerful exercise. Just about everything I had on those walls came true. I still use this practice today, although I don't paste pictures on walls anymore. Now it's your turn. This is what I do today, and this is what I'd suggest you do too.

Get a large bulletin board or find a cardboard box big enough for this exercise. I have used both a box and a bulletin board. When first getting started, you may want to stay with the bulletin board because it can be placed in your line of vision.

Go through magazines and cut out pictures that speak to you. They can be material things, relationships that you want to have, things you want to do or become (a great golfer), or who you want to be (more spiritual, more centered and at peace). If you are using a bulletin board, put the pictures on it. They can overlap. Keep the board in your sight, either on the wall or floor by your desk. If it's in a box, then keep that near you so you can go through it and look at the pictures daily.

Practice #2: Know Your Rights

Do you have the right to have the items and desires that you posted on your board?

Wallace Wattles would say yes! In 1903 he wrote *The Science of Getting Rich*,[2] a practical book on how to get rich. Wattles claims that if you read his book and follow what he tells you, you will certainly become rich. I, too, would suggest that you read his book, especially chapter one, "The Right to be Rich."

Wattles states, "There is nothing wrong in wanting to get rich. The desire for riches is really the desire for a richer, fuller, and more abundant life; and that desire is praiseworthy."

This is an important statement which will stir various feelings.

Ask yourself, "Do you think you have the right to be rich?" Explore your thoughts and prejudices. What types of judgments do you place on the person who walks in to the supermarket with a mink coat, dripping in diamonds? Or how about the guy who pulls up to the restaurant in a Ferrari? Do you envision their lives? Do you think about where they probably live? Do you wonder what they do for a living or if they even work? Do you assume that they come from money? Look at these thoughts honestly, as well as your judgments about poor people. Do you assume the homeless person you pass on the street will spend any money they get on alcohol? Do you wonder if they held a good job before they became homeless?

You may think that Wattles' statement is bold and arrogant. This may be exactly where you can begin some work on how you hold the thought of having lots of money and deserving it. Explore these questions with a good friend or coach.

> Do you know people who are rich?
> What thoughts do you have about them?
> Do you ever pass people who live on the streets?
> What do you tell yourself about them?
> Who could you help if *you* were really rich?

Marianne Williamson wrote a poem about our deepest fears. In it she writes that what frightens us most is not that we are *not enough*, but that we are powerful beyond belief, and yet afraid to show it, even to ourselves. It's not necessarily our fears and insecurities that hold us back, she states, but untamed thoughts of being wildly brilliant and talented.

Is it possible that we are fearful of being our authentic, glorious selves? After all, if we stand in our own glory, others may judge us for being too *out there*, too wealthy, or too extravagant. How many times have you held back, not wanting to show yourself, concerned about the judgments of others? Could we actually be afraid of our own light? Perhaps so. Think about it. If you really *got* how magnificent you were, in all respects, and how much you have to offer others—others who actually yearn to learn more about you, it may be too big to truly let in.

Williamson states that we all have the right to have everything that we desire. We have the right to let our light shine strong.

The following is a quote from her poem that may motivate you, as it does me, to let your internal light shine bright.

"And as we let our own light shine, we unconsciously give other people permission to do the same. As we're liberated from our own fear, our presence automatically liberates others."[3]

When you stand in your own perfection, others around you will rise up to do the same. That's what I call freedom.

Post this where you can see it and read it every day.

Now ask yourself again, "Do I have the right, or do I deserve, to get everything that I desire?"

You do!

Work on this practice until you can say yes. When you do, you're on your way to following in JJ's tracks.

Practice #3: Identify Standards You Live By

What standards do you live by? Is education important? Love? Family? Money? Happiness? Health? Most people would answer yes to all of these.

Make a list of what is important to you. Are you at your peak of satisfaction? Is everything working perfectly? It's doubtful you'd give a 100 percent to most of them. There's always room for growth.

Circle the top five items on your list. Post them where you can see them. You don't have to put them in any order. It may look like this:

> Family
> Love
> Self-development
> Money
> Health

Take care of yourself first in each of these areas. When you take care of yourself first, you can serve others from your overflow. You can serve them with joy.

Beside each standard, write down what you want to get. For example:

> Family: See my grandchild weekly.
> Love: Love myself . . . always.
> Self-development: Write books.
> Money: Have $10 million dollars at retirement
> Health: Cut out white flour and sugar.

Here's the fun part. This is the secret to JJ's success. Beside each standard, write down what you will give to others.

> Family: Really be present and listen when one of them is talking.
> Love: Show it in my eyes when I'm talking to them.
> Self-development: Suggest books or courses for others.
> Money: Donate 10 percent of my income this year to my favorite causes.
> Health: Help my daughter to exercise more.

Now you have identified your standards and given thought to what you want and what you want to give to others. It's time to go live them.

Practice #4: Live Your Standards

For the next two weeks write an action statement beside each standard, every day. You will work with this statement during your day. Write it the night before and get up in the morning ready to take it on.

> Family: Leave a message on my brother's cell phone telling him I love him.
> Love: Send flowers to my husband. Just because.
> Self-development: Read a chapter on creating joy.
> Money: Give away $5 today to a good cause. If I don't come across one (which I'm sure I will), put it in my donation box on my desk.
> Health: Give up sugar today.

Notice that they don't have to be hard. You can make them as simple as you wish. But be sure to fulfill them. Each day will have a new list, although you can duplicate a prior action if you'd like. An example would be health: give up sugar today. You may want to continue using that each day for the next two weeks.

Practice #5: Go Back Home in Times of Question

Like JJ, we all get confronted by dilemmas at one time or another. There are small ones that test our values like being undercharged for an item you purchase. Do you tell the cashier? Or do you just walk away knowing that you got one over on them?

Then there are the bigger dilemmas, like the one JJ faced. When his people were not given the bonuses he promised them by the acquiring company, he could have gotten angry, thrown his arms up in the air, and told his management team, "I tried to get it for you, but they just wouldn't budge."

Or he could go into his own pocket and pay them from his personal account, which is, of course, just what JJ did.

Sometimes our dilemmas can really take us off track, hindering judgment and having us question our standards. JJ was quite clear on his, so the decision made was swift. He could then get on with his life.

When you get stuck on what is the right thing to do, you now have a guide. Go back to your list of standards. Read through them. Look at what you wrote down as your desires about getting and receiving from the standards you set. Can you find the answer to your dilemma listed within the standards you've written?

Let the list guide you to make good decisions. You've done the hard work of identifying your standards or values. When faced with a difficult decision, revert back to your list for the answers. It will save you hours of angst and give you more time to do what you love to do, which I'm sure doesn't include worrying.

SUMMARY

☑ Find and cut out pictures that represent what you want to get, what you want to do, and who you want to be.
☑ Post those pictures or gather them into a box. Put them in daily view.
☑ Identify and work through any doubts you have on the right to receive what you desire.
☑ Shine brightly. Playing small doesn't suit anyone.
☑ Rely on your standards (values) for living when faced with a dilemma
☑ Use your list of standards to get what you most desire and help you with decisions that involve integrity.
☑ Use your list of standards to give to others the things you value most.

NOTES

1. Junior Achievement, http://www.ja.org/about/about.shtml.
2. Wallace Wattles, *The Science of Getting Rich* (BN Publishing, 2008).
3. Marianne Williamson, *A Return to Love: Reflection on the Principles of A Course in Miracles* (New York: HarperCollins, 2006).

Appendices

APPENDIX A: ENTREPRENEURIAL FITNESS QUIZ

Although I personally use these practices daily and have benefited greatly from incorporating them into my life, each person's outcome will be different. A lot depends on where you are starting from with your current habits. I must insert a disclaimer here. There are no guarantees that this will work for you or that you'll achieve results indicated or any other results. Each person is different and much has to do with your physical and mental condition upon embarking on this course. I am not a medical doctor or psychologist and I'm not qualified to provide you with that type of information. Please check with your medical advisor or psychologist before starting any of these practices.

Directions:

    A. Rate each item 1–10; 10 being the most satisfied.
    B. If not a 10, explain what is missing for it not to be at a 10.
    C. List actions needed to get you to a 10.
    D. Commit to a date that the actions will be completed.

Let's use #1 as an example, with Anne's answers.

Example (Anne)

---
1. Physical Exam (annual checkup, blood work, etc.)
    A. Rating: 5
    B. What's missing? I haven't been to see a doctor in over 5 years.
    C. Actions: Make appointment. Get exam. Get blood work. Talk about stomach pains and migraines.
    D. Date to be completed: October 31
---

1. Physical Exam (annual checkup, blood work, etc.)

    A. Rating:
    B. What's missing?
    C. Actions:
    D. Date to be completed:

2. Eye Exam

    A. Rating:
    B. What's missing?
    C. Actions:
    D. Date to be completed:

3. Dental Exam

    A. Rating:
    B. What's missing?
    C. Actions:
    D. Date to be completed:

4. Mammogram (where applicable)

    A. Rating:
    B. What's missing?
    C. Actions:
    D. Date to be completed:

5. Gynecological or Prostate Exam (where applicable)

    A. Rating:
    B. What's missing?
    C. Actions:
    D. Date to be completed:

6. Colonoscopy (where applicable)

    A. Rating:
    B. What's missing?
    C. Actions:
    D. Date to be completed:

7. Nutrition and Diet

    A. Rating:
    B. What's missing?
    C. Actions:
    D. Date to be completed:

8. Sleep (well-rested)

    A. Rating:
    B. What's missing?
    C. Actions:
    D. Date to be completed:

9. Exercise and Physical Activity
   A. Rating:
   B. What's missing?
   C. Actions:
   D. Date to be completed:

10. Mind-Clearing Exercises and Relaxation, such as meditation, yoga, tai chi, or qigong
    A. Rating:
    B. What's missing?
    C. Actions:
    D. Date to be completed:

11. Addiction-Free, such as: food, alcohol, drugs, tobacco, shopping, gambling, sex, work, etc.
    A. Rating:
    B. What's missing?
    C. Actions:
    D. Date to be completed:

12. House/Home Environment
    A. Rating:
    B. What's missing?
    C. Actions:
    D. Date to be completed:

13. Office(s)
    A. Rating:
    B. What's missing?
    C. Actions:
    D. Date to be completed:

14. Car
    A. Rating:
    B. What's missing?
    C. Actions:
    D. Date to be completed:

15. Dress and Grooming—inclusive of your clothes, shoes, jewelry, make-up, hair, nails, briefcase, handbags, glasses, etc.
    A. Rating:
    B. What's missing?
    C. Actions:
    D. Date to be completed:

16. Outstanding Bills (personal) and Accounts Payable (business)
    A. Rating:
    B. What's missing?
    C. Actions:
    D. Date to be completed:

17. Unresolved Legal Matters

    A. Rating:
    B. What's missing?
    C. Actions:
    D. Date to be completed:

18. Financial Debt

    A. Rating:
    B. What's missing?
    C. Actions:
    D. Date to be completed:

19. Your Credit Rating

    A. Rating:
    B. What's missing?
    C. Actions:
    D. Date to be completed:

20. Tax and Financial Records Organized

    A. Rating:
    B. What's missing?
    C. Actions:
    D. Date to be completed:

21. Bank Accounts Reconciled

    A. Rating:
    B. What's missing?
    C. Actions:
    D. Date to be completed:

22. Income Taxes Prepared/Filed

    A. Rating:
    B. What's missing?
    C. Actions:
    D. Date to be completed:

23. Investments (retirement, college, wealth-building, etc.)

    A. Rating:
    B. What's missing?
    C. Actions:
    D. Date to be completed:

24. Outstanding Gifts and Cards

    A. Rating:
    B. What's missing?
    C. Actions:
    D. Date to be completed:

25. Phone Calls (to be returned)

    A. Rating:
    B. What's missing?
    C. Actions:
    D. Date to be completed:

26. E-mails (to be answered)

    A. Rating:
    B. What's missing?
    C. Actions:
    D. Date to be completed:

27. Borrowed Items (to be returned)

    A. Rating:
    B. What's missing?
    C. Actions:
    D. Date to be completed:

28. Items Borrowed by Others (to be returned to you)

    A. Rating:
    B. What's missing?
    C. Actions:
    D. Date to be completed:

29. Up-to-Date Agreements Made with Others

    A. Rating:
    B. What's missing?
    C. Actions:
    D. Date to be completed:

30. Unresolved Employee Conversations/Issues

    A. Rating:
    B. What's missing?
    C. Actions:
    D. Date to be completed:

31. Unresolved Client/Customer Conversations/Issues

    A. Rating:
    B. What's missing?
    C. Actions:
    D. Date to be completed:

32. Unresolved Vendor Conversations/Issues

    A. Rating:
    B. What's missing?
    C. Actions:
    D. Date to be completed:

33. Unresolved Professional Advisor (accountant, lawyer, board member, consultant or coach, etc.) Conversations/Issues

    A. Rating:
    B. What's missing?
    C. Actions:
    D. Date to be completed:

34. Spiritual Well-Being

    A. Rating:
    B. What's missing?
    C. Actions:
    D. Date to be completed:

35. Energy Balance

    A. Rating:
    B. What's missing?
    C. Actions:
    D. Date to be completed:

36. Anything else

    A. Rating:
    B. What's missing?
    C. Actions:
    D. Date to be completed:

After completing the Entrepreneurial Fitness Quiz, circle all items that you've rated seven or lower. Next choose three of those items and put a star after each one. For each starred item imagine you've taken the necessary actions to raise the rating to a 10. Even though it hasn't happened yet, imagine it has. How does that feel? Are you free of worry, guilt, or anxiety? Do you feel healthier or reassured?

Now you're ready to go for it. Take those three items and implement the actions you've listed. Give yourself a short time period to complete them. Perhaps it is just two days. Although you may not be able to visit the doctor for your annual check-up in two days, you've taken the action to make the appointment. After you've completed those three starred items, do the same thing again with three more items. Continue through your list at a quick pace. Perhaps you can set an overall goal to complete the actions on your entire list within two weeks.

Don't forget when you've completed going through your list to congratulate yourself for taking care of YOU!

APPENDIX B: ACTION PLAN

See Chapter 9, Step 5 for Lisa's example.

1. Write your goal in simple format.

A goal has three elements: What you want, by when, and how you'll know you got there.

2. In order of priority, list the three *greatest* challenges you are currently facing around that goal.

A.

B.

C.

3. List two areas of personal self-growth that will support reaching your goal.

A.

B.

4. Considering you had all the resources and support, what is the *number one greatest change* you would like to make to your:

Give a separate answer for each.

A. Life as a whole

B. Physical self, your health and well being

C. Intellectual, mental self

D. Emotional, spiritual self

E. Work life

F. Family life

G. Social relationships outside of work

H. Relationship with time

I. Relationship with money

J. Relationship with yourself

K. Leadership team (if applicable)

L. Partners (if applicable)

M. Peers

N. Employees or vendors

O. Company

6. As best as you can, describe where you will be/want to be with your goal, in:

A. One year:

B. Two years:

C. Three years:

D. Five years:

7. For each year above in question #6, write a short plan with five steps to make it happen. *I don't know* is not an answer.

A. One year:

B. Two years:

C. Three years:

D. Five years

Index

About the Author

NANCI RAPHAEL developed a groundbreaking approach for entrepreneurs and business leaders to grow their businesses across multiple bottom lines: professional and personal development, financial growth, and impact on the lives of the people they serve and the world around them. Recognized as an award winning entrepreneur, a luminary in business and leadership coaching, author, and teacher, she is also the founder and CEO of Leadership & Executive Development, LLC (keyleaders.com) and Voom Factor (voomfactor.com). Ms. Raphael has worked with business leaders in Fortune 500 companies, family-owned businesses, and entrepreneurial enterprises. She is married and has 3 children.